Graduate to a
GREAT
JOB

Make Your
College Degree Pay Off
in TODAY'S Market

DAVID DeLONG

Graduate to a Great Job: Make Your College Degree Pay Off in Today's Market
by David DeLong

This book is designed to provide accurate and authoritative information in regard to the
subject matter covered. It is sold with the understanding that the publisher is not engaged
in rendering legal, accounting, or other professional services. If legal advice or other expert
assistance is required, the services of a competent professional should be sought.

Published by Longstone Press
60 Thoreau Street, Suite 284
Concord, MA 01742
www.GraduateToAGreatJob.com

ISBN: 978-0-9888686-0-1
Library of Congress Control Number: 2013905993

Library of Congress Cataloging-in-Publication Data

DeLong, David
        Graduate to a great job: make your college degree pay off in today's market
                p.   cm.
        Includes bibliographic references and index
        ISBN: 978-0-9888686-0-1
        1. Business/Economics   2. Careers   3. Job Hunting

Longstone Press books may be purchased in quantity by contacting the publisher directly.

Cover design: Priscilla Sturges & Nick Zelinger
Interior design: Nick Zelinger, www.NZGraphics.com
Editing: Anne Morrissey

10 9 8 7 6 5 4 3 2 1

First Edition

Printed in the United States

For Sue, Sara, and Anna,
whose love and creative spirit still takes my breath away.

Table of Contents

The Big Picture

The pain and pleasure of finding meaningful work today.

Introduction

In case you haven't noticed, it's very hard for today's graduates to get a great job coming out of college. This is especially true for students graduating with liberal arts degrees.

What does it take to land a great job? Ask grads who've done it, and most will tell you, "You'd be surprised."

"I Should Be You!"

She was working the lunch shift in a busy Pittsburgh beer bar when the call came. Laura took the phone from her apron and glanced around at the ten tables she was covering. The caller ID indicated it was a prominent technology company where she had recently interviewed. She was afraid to get her hopes up as she ran to the bathroom to take the call.

Since graduating from Lehigh University more than two years ago, Laura had applied for at least 100 jobs where she might use the writing skills from her journalism degree. But all she had to show for her efforts was an endless string of rejections and four waitressing jobs. She recalls:

> I was so frustrated with the whole process. You work so hard. You do everything right. I was sick of waiting on tables. At happy hour I'd wait on people my own age who looked successful, and I'd think, "I should be you!"

Then in a moment, she was. Standing in the ladies room of that Pittsburgh bar, the cell phone pressed to her ear, Laura finally got what she had been waiting for—a job offer from a company she really wanted to work for. She remembers the moment clearly:

3

I did everything my Dad said not to do. He always told me to look over an offer first. But once I heard that I had the job, I didn't even listen to what the person was saying. I accepted right away. I walked back onto the floor and shouted, "I got a job!" I looked at my manager and said, "I'm quitting in two weeks." He smiled and said, "You gotta finish your shift first."

Things Didn't Go as Planned

Carl had moved to Minneapolis to be with his girlfriend a few months after graduating from Colorado College with an economics degree. He was confident he'd land a job soon, even though he had limited experience, no prospects, and no network in his new city.

I thought I was a hotshot. I had a great internship after my junior year. I had a good resume. But I was delusional about what employers are looking for. People wanted experience, and all I could give them was a motivated, smart recruit. I didn't even know how to prepare for an interview!

Now, more than a year later, Carl still didn't have a job, despite his extensive networking, interviewing, and looking for opportunities in the finance industry. But things were looking up. He recently had second-round interviews in three large companies. Then one morning he got a call from a prominent investment management firm. Carl remembers:

The guy on the phone said they wanted to make me a job offer. I was speechless. It had been such a long time. I was thrilled because I didn't think I connected that well with my interviewer there. I accepted the offer immediately and began thinking about all the people I'd have to thank. I knew now the networking would never stop.

Screaming in Spokane

It was a beautiful summer evening in Spokane. Maria and her fiancé, Jeff, had his parents over for dinner on the patio in the backyard. Since graduating from nearby Eastern Washington University over a year ago, she had developed an excellent reputation as a substitute teacher. Still, Maria was unable to find a full-time position. Recently, she had interviewed for a first-grade teaching job, the last opening for the coming school year in Spokane. More than 400 people had applied, and she was one of only four candidates interviewed. Her phone rang during dinner. Maria recalls:

> *I loved teaching, but I was thinking I didn't go to school for four years to be a substitute teacher. I was burned out on subbing. Then the principal is on the phone and she asks me if I got the message she left two hours ago. She said they wanted to offer me the position. And, you know, suddenly I'm screaming, standing in the back yard, jumping up and down! I'm trying to be professional, but I finally had a teaching job. I called my Mom right away. It was a great moment.*

Time to Start Writing Your Own Happy Ending

Succeeding in today's job market means knowing what works—and what doesn't. Despite all the bad news in the media and the negative talk among your friends and parents, remember this: a*lmost half of new college grads are getting jobs they feel good about after finishing school!* The purpose of this book is to make sure you end up in that group of graduates who feel good about how their career is starting out. OK, maybe you won't have the "perfect" job, but it'll be a good beginning.

This book is based on real-life case studies. Every lesson, every piece of advice was gleaned from or verified by more than 30 recent college grads I interviewed who successfully landed their first job. In a few cases, the journey was relatively short. In most cases, it was incredibly long and difficult. But every story ended well. (All names have been disguised.)

This book is designed to give you—and your parents—hope. You *can* get a good job! Laura, Carl, and Maria all landed fine jobs, eventually. **Your story will have a happy ending, too, if you follow the strategies and tactics used by this group of creative, persistent, and proactive young grads.**

Graduate to a Great Job will help you no matter what your circumstances may be.

- *Are you a junior or senior in college headed into the full-time job market for the first time?* This book is loaded with examples and tips on how to make progress each day to land a job you want.

- *Are you a recent college grad whose job search has stalled or who is back in the job market a few years after graduation?* My research shows that those who get a job quickly after finishing school often find themselves looking again in a year or two. And that second or third job search can be even harder. The lessons learned in this book will show you how to get the traction you'll need to get back in the game—and off your parents' couch.

- *Are you a first- or second-year college student?* Here, you'll find a guide for making smarter decisions through college to set you up for a more productive job search in a couple of years. This advice comes from grads who had fun in college and still succeeded afterwards.

- *Finally, are you a parent whose child fits any of the categories above?* Chapter 18 is written just for you! (I'm the parent of a college student, too, and frankly the entire book is written with a parent's hopes and concerns in mind.) You'll find loads of ideas about how you can help your children jump-start their career. *Graduate to a Great Job* is a terrific conversation starter and resource that you can share with young adults to give you *both* hope and actionable ideas for getting that great job faster!

How to Use This Book

Graduate to a Great Job gives you lots of practical things you can do immediately. These steps are summarized at the end of most chapters as a "Checklist for Action."

How you read this book—from start to finish, or by choosing topics that are particularly interesting—is up to you. But nothing you read will change your career prospects *unless you take action and start doing things differently!*

Here's an overview of the chapters. You can decide where to jump in. Need more information on topics like networking, effective online research, or creating resumes? Use the additional links I've provided to the most up-to-date resources.

The Big Picture. Chapter 1 explains why new college grads must work much harder today to launch their careers. Skip this chapter if you're already in the middle of a job search and just want practical ideas. But it is important for understanding why finding meaningful work has become such a challenge. You also will see the variety of successful recent grads—their schools, majors, and employers—whose stories are the heart of this book.

Focusing Your Search. Chapters 2 and 3 address the most challenging question facing many students today: what kind of work do I want to do? If you can't answer that question, start here. Chapter 4 provides stories of how two students struggled to figure out what their first jobs should be. If you already know the type of job you want, go to Chapter 5. It shows how to assess yourself against the competition and will keep you from wasting time applying for positions where you don't have a prayer.

Building Experience. Chapters 6-8 explain how to land great internships and make sure they payoff in your post-college job search. Even if you have graduated, check out the section on post-grad internships. Then read Chapter 9 for other ideas about building your experience base.

Making Connections. Networking in today's crazy-busy work environment is the most critical skill you'll need to build your career after college. And what if you're an introvert? It's all covered in Chapters 10-12.

Using Technology. Can you pass the technology IQ test in Chapter 13? What you don't know about job-search technologies will keep you unemployed today. And Chapter 14 shows how to use particular social media applications so you'll stand out from the other one million-plus new grads this year.

Selling Yourself. Landing a great job is about convincing employers that you are the best solution to their problem. Expectations for resumes and job interviews have changed dramatically. Chapters 15 and 16 show how to use these tools to your advantage.

Career Services. Chapter 17 explains how to get the most out of your school's career center and offers insights career counselors are afraid to tell you.

Modern Family. Chapter 18 shows how Mom and Dad can help you get employed faster without being a pain in the butt.

Lessons Learned & Happy Endings. In Chapter 19 recent grads share what they wish they had known before they started their post-college job search. Chapter 20 describes what it will look and feel like to finally land the job you want.

Special Section: Stories of Search Strategies That Paid Off. The last section of *Graduate to a Great Job* shows how successful grads worked through specific challenges in their search. Start here if you like learning from other people's stories about using internships strategically, building effective job search networks, leveraging technology, and nailing a job interview.

This book is intended to give you and your parents the confidence and the tools you need to find meaningful work in today's tough job market. Others have done it. So can you. It won't be easy. In fact, it may be the hardest thing you've ever done, but the rewards will be huge.

This is your time. It's your life. Go for it!

CHAPTER ONE

Why is Finding a Good Job After College So Tough?

E very generation of college graduates faces challenges breaking into the job market. If you're thinking you have it tougher than your parents did, you have no idea how right you are. The fact is, today's grads actually face the worst job market in decades.

Studies show a whopping 54% of recent college grads are either unemployed or underemployed. And even if you're one of the lucky ones who lined up a good job right out of school, don't think you're home free. The average tenure of employees hired today is 1.5 years, so chances are you, too, will be in the job market again soon. If you don't believe these numbers, just check with friends who graduated a few years before you. My research shows that many students who land their first post-college job pretty easily find themselves struggling to get that second or third job a few years later.

The purpose of telling you this is not to send you into panic mode, but rather to motivate you to pay more attention to the elements of a successful job search today. There are, in fact, smart ways to navigate recent changes in the job market, so you end up with a great job and a promising future. And these solutions aren't impossibly hard or expensive. You can do this! But landing a good job today starts with understanding how the job-search game has changed and why you need to invest extra effort in finding work after graduation. In this chapter you'll learn:

- The four factors that make finding post-college employment one of the toughest things you've ever done.

- Good news about the value of your college degree in today's job market.

- How to use your understanding of these big changes in the job market to your advantage.

Here are four reasons why getting hired as a recent college grad has gotten much harder. Understand these factors and you'll be better prepared to apply the tools and strategies needed to get you employed faster.

1. The Economic "Big Picture" Keeps Employers From Hiring

Uncertainty about the future is a bad thing when companies, as well as nonprofits and government agencies, are deciding whether to take on new employees. No business wants to hire people if it is about to go in the tank.

Threats like the European debt crisis and China's slowing economic growth have left lots of executives holding their breath, unsure about the potential negative impacts on their business. And, in case you haven't noticed, the president and Congress haven't exactly been getting along. There are ongoing questions about whether leaders in Washington will ever reach agreement on how to cut the huge U.S. budget deficit.

Those kingpins of late-night news—Jon Stewart and Stephen Colbert—have great fun spinning these issues for our entertainment. But, in reality, these uncertainties make lots of companies very nervous about the future. And when managers are nervous, they are cautious about hiring.

Another factor is there are simply fewer jobs out there today. In fact, the U.S. needs to add seven million jobs just to get back to where we were before the Great Recession of 2008-2009. Some experts say this serious jobs deficit will last at least until 2020. The problem is made worse for college grads because most of the jobs added since the recession are low-wage jobs, not the kinds of positions you want to pursue with a college degree.

Combine these factors with the long-standing trend to ship jobs overseas to lower-wage countries like China and India. Then throw in budget deficits at all levels of government, which led the public sector to cut more than 500,000 jobs in the last three years. This includes positions ranging from teachers to policy analysts to park rangers. Add it all up and you've got a U.S. workforce that's not growing nearly fast enough to absorb all the talented young people coming out of college today.

2. This Ain't Your Parents' Workplace

Baby boomers and Gen-Xers may not like to hear this, but the skills required to work for companies today are much more complicated than 20 years ago. That's because organizations have become:

- *Increasingly dependent on using more sophisticated technologies* —e.g. "Do you have experience with electronic medical records, computer-aided design systems, Salesforce.com, or data warehousing?"

- *More ethnically and generationally diverse*—e.g. "Can you work with a bunch of veteran engineers scattered around the world for whom English is a second language?"

- *Interdependent with other organizations, such as suppliers and partners*—e.g. "Of course, you'll be working with suppliers in India and with partners you've never met."

- *Incredibly focused on controlling costs*—e.g. "Nobody has had a raise around here in four years, and they just cut our marketing budget by 10 percent."

This means the jobs you're likely to be interested in are more demanding and fast changing than they would have been a few decades ago, if those jobs even existed. One veteran director of career services explained it this way:

Companies today are looking for multi-skilled, multi-talented people. They don't just want you to have a strong technical skill set, for example. They also need you to be able to work as part of a team, to be sensitive to cultural diversity and able to work with people who have a different first language.

Gone are the days when employers viewed new recruits as an investment in the future, and they would train you in exchange for your loyalty. Companies today want more than potential and a good attitude. They're looking for experience and demonstrated capabilities. And hiring managers also know you're probably not going to stay very long. This makes them more hesitant to invest in training new hires.

3. Welcome to the Hiring Process from Hell

In addition to wanting you to have more skills, organizations also do three things that make getting a full-time, grown-up job harder than it used to be.

Let's start with the automated screening of resumes. Applicant Tracking Systems (ATS) are now routinely used to review resumes to decide who gets considered for an interview. (See Chapter 13 for how to deal with them.) These systems are automated to the point of absurdity. If your resume doesn't have the right key words and phrases for a specific job, it will be ignored. Think I'm kidding?

Donald Asher, author of one of my favorite books, Cracking the Hidden Job Market, *submitted a bogus resume from Rex, an ace guard dog, to several corporate websites. Rex had great qualifications, which included "guarding warehouses and junkyards."*

He also was "able to bite unauthorized personnel in the buttocks if they failed to show appropriate identification." Best of all, Rex asked to be paid in "kibbles," his favorite dog food.

So, you ask, just how automated is the application process? Rex the dog got a cordial set of email responses to his application assuring him that the firms were carefully "comparing his qualifications and experiences to (our) staffing needs."

You can laugh or cry at the absurdity of letting computers decide whether you're worth an interview. But if you don't know the new rules of the technology-driven hiring game, you're at a serious disadvantage. (By the way, unless your parents work in human resources or have looked for a job recently, they won't know about ATS technologies. It has changed the job-search process dramatically.)

"Alternative work arrangements" are the new normal. More and more, employers are structuring jobs for contractors (read: no benefits, no commitment) or part-time freelancing arrangements, or as internships—paid and unpaid. (See Chapter 6 to learn how internships are changing.) This is a strategy for keeping costs down, responding to an uncertain economic environment and screening potential new hires before taking them on full-time. Disney alone is reported to use 8,000 interns. A pharmaceutical company like Pfizer has hundreds of internships available to people enrolled in school for the following semester. Microsoft and Google are well known for using internships to screen potential new hires.

There's lots of debate these days about whether companies are abusing internship programs to get free or very cheap labor. A study by Intern Bridge, a firm that helps big companies design internship programs, found that in 2011 77% of unpaid interns had to take second jobs to get by. Big surprise! Certainly some organizations are violating the spirit of how interns should be used. But the reality is if you want a good job in today's market, you're going to have to play along to get the experience you need.

Depending on the field you're going into, you may have to consider taking a job as a contractor or freelancer. It's standard practice, for example, in advertising and television production. Or an internship may seem like your only option after graduation, if you don't have enough experience. If you know ahead of time how jobs are structured in particular fields today, you can develop more realistic expectations about opportunities and salaries in those fields you're pursuing

Getting hired can take freakin' forever. Many organizations have gone through significant "downsizing" in recent years. (That's the polite way of saying, "We fired a bunch of people to save money.") What this means for you is that most companies today are understaffed and everyone is incredibly busy, so scheduling interviews can be a nightmare.

Because companies are operating so lean, managers are more scared than ever of making hiring mistakes: bringing in just one "bad apple" can disrupt the entire team's chemistry. Hiring a loser is incredibly demoralizing to people who already feel they're working their asses off to keep the organization going. So managers are much more cautious about avoiding hiring mistakes. This means getting a formal job offer can be a painfully long process.

Are you getting the picture now? Oh, there's one more thing.

4. You've Got More Competition Than Ever

In 2012, 1.7 million students graduated from college in the U.S. When you attempt to enter today's job market, you're not only competing against those in your own college class, but also those who have graduated a few years ahead of you. Many of your older friends from college are still trying to launch their careers. In addition, Gen-Ys in their late twenties are likely to be back in the job market, either because they were laid off or couldn't stand their previous job. They may have an advantage over you, too—their recent work experience is often highly valued by managers doing the hiring.

Of course, most everyone you know coming out of college has the added pressure of college loans to pay off. The average total debt for students leaving college today is over $23,000. That level of debt has increased 47% in the last decade. So when you're looking for work in the next few years, you have more competition from experienced people, everyone needs the money to pay those loans and their smartphone bills, and the salaries offered will likely be less than in past years. In fact, you're probably competing for jobs that are paying salaries worth 5% less than what new college grads were receiving ten years ago.

Summing Up: Barriers to Your Successful Job Search

So here's the situation you're facing when looking for a job today:

- Employers are hesitant to hire because of the big-picture economic threats to their business.

- There are fewer good jobs today than there were five years ago.

- Companies expect new hires to have more experience and skills than ever.

- Employers are more likely to fill roles by offering internships, part-time jobs, or contractor arrangements without benefits and a long-term commitment.

- Because organizations are short-staffed and everyone is crazy-busy, the hiring process can take forever.

- There's more competition for jobs that pay less to cover your increased expenses.

Believe it or not, you're actually in a good place. If things sound tough, consider the alternative. What if you hadn't gone to college? Sure, you wouldn't have those loans to worry about, and all that goofy furniture. And your list of Facebook friends would only be half what it is today. But guess what kind of future you'd be looking at without a college degree?

If you've graduated from high school since 2008, but did not go to college, there's only a 16% chance you're working full-time today. Those jobs at Burger King and Forever 21 are looking pretty sweet. Whatever complaints you have about being underemployed or frustrated in your job search, at least you're in the game. Your situation is a hell of a lot worse if you don't have a college degree. In the last 30 years, the earnings gap between high-school graduates and college-educated adults has tripled. Do look on the bright side. You can expect to make more than twice as much in wages over your working life as your friends who never paid college tuition.

But gone are the days when a college degree guaranteed a good job and a solid income for life. Finding meaningful work that pays a wage you can be happy with is going to be a constant challenge throughout your career.

Just by reading this chapter, you now know more than most Gen-Ys about why your job search is going to be, or already is, so challenging. And you can use your knowledge of how the job market has changed to your advantage. There's no reason to panic. What you need is an organized approach, along with realistic expectations about what success will look like. You *can* do this! And this book is going to help. A lot.

Exhibit 1-1 (pages 20-21) shows a list of the recent grads who provided inspiration for this book. These Gen-Ys are just like you. They are from big universities and small colleges all around the country. They all finished their undergraduate degrees in the last few years, many in liberal arts. And, in the process, they persevered and landed a good—or even great—job. This book is based on their stories, struggles, and lessons learned. Some had an easier time than others. But none were handed a job or had employers recruiting them. Every person in this book has overcome obstacles to launch their career. You can benefit from what they have learned. Let's get started.

Exhibit 1-1: Meet 32 Who Graduated to Great Jobs

Name	Job	College	Major
Dirk	Associate editor, online news	American University	Journalism
Indira	Medical training & development specialist	Baylor University	Psychology/Spanish
Sara	Development associate, arts nonprofit	Beloit College	Sociology
Ethan	Associate director, educational nonprofit	Beloit College	Sociology & Sound Design
Carmen	Marketing assistant, high tech	Boston University	Public Relations
Andrew	High-school drama teacher	Bowdoin College	English & Theatre Arts
Tobias	Google (contractor)	Brandeis University	Computer Science & Economics
Zoey	Event planning coordinator	Central Michigan University	Recreation
Luke	Examiner, Federal Reserve Bank	Christopher Newport University	Philosophy & Economics
Zach	Junior associate, commercial real estate	Colby College	History
Carl	Portfolio administrator, investment management	Colorado College	Economics
Maria	Elementary school teacher	Eastern Washington University	Education
Ryan	Investment analyst	Fordham University	Finance
Olivia	Marketing coordinator, social-media software	Georgetown University	Psychology
Faith	Web & graphics designer	James Madison University	Graphic Design & Business Comm.
Laura	Research associate, global technology	Lehigh University	Journalism
Tyler	Public relations coordinator	Louisiana State University	Mass Communication
Ling	NASA software engineer	Massachusetts Institute of Technology	Aerospace Engineering & Theater

Exhibit 1-1: Meet 32 Who Graduated to Great Jobs (continued)

Name	Job	College	Major
Daniel	Paralegal, U.S. Department of Justice	Pennsylvania State University	Political Science
Brooke	Online community manager, education website	University of California, Berkeley	Sociology
Anna	Women's health advocate, community health agency	University of California, Los Angeles	Political Science
Lily	Online advertising manager, education website	University of California, Santa Barbara	Art History
Molly	Process engineer, automotive parts manufacturing	University of Colorado, Boulder	Mechanical Engineering
Yong	Consultant, IT services	University of Florida	Mechanical Engineering
Taylor	Investment banking assistant	University of Illinois at Urbana-Champaign	Psychology
Carlos	City Year, middle-school tutor & mentor	University of Maryland	Cell Biology & Genetics
Madison	Research assistant, Memorial Sloan-Kettering Cancer Center	University of Michigan	Psychology
Lee	Management trainee, Enterprise Rent-A-Car	University of Ontario Institute of Technology	Accounting
Katherine	Sales rep, wine distributor	University of Texas at Austin	Communications
Marco	Marketing coordinator, Walt Disney	University of Texas at Austin	Communications
Lucas	Freelance TV production	University of Texas at Austin	Film
Pablo	Account manager, financial research firm	Union College	Economics & Philosophy

21

Checklist for Action:
Assess Your Current Situation

Now you know the barriers you face in finding a job. But you also know that some recent grads have succeeded in finding work they enjoy. So how do you make sure you end up in this group? First, check your current emotional state in terms of your post-college career. Where are you today?

A. Just beginning to think about getting a job.

B. In denial because I don't want college to end and getting a job looks impossible.

C. Panicked or frustrated because I don't know what to do.

D. Already taking action and anxious to make more progress on my search.

E. Frustrated and depressed because I've graduated and can't find a job I like.

You have classmates and friends in each of these categories, and that's okay. But it's not okay to stay there. As one famous career coach likes to say, "What got you here, won't get you there." You've got to start doing things differently. For starters, take the three steps below.

___1. Set a goal for when you want to have a full time job after graduating. At graduation? End of the summer? By next Christmas? As soon as possible? Are you taking into account how long your job search will probably take? (Assume about eight months.)

____**2. Decide when you're going to start a serious, organized job-search process like the steps outlined in this book.** It may be fall of senior year, or not until after graduation. It's up to you. But don't kid yourself. The longer you delay, the more time after graduation you'll spend feeling frustrated and answering those annoying questions from your parents' friends.

____**3. Have a conversation with your parents to make sure they have a realistic understanding of the challenges you face in finding a good job.** They're probably more anxious than you realize about your job prospects. But they don't necessarily know how to help you. Have a conversation with them using the key points in this chapter, so they understand this is not the job market they once knew. You're not trying to upset them, but you need to set their expectations, too. Also, it will become evident in this book that some tactics, which worked in their past job searches, are probably useless today. Others, however, such as networking, are still highly valuable. Your parents can almost certainly help you there.

Find Focus
& Gain Experience

Learn by doing: it's the key to finding work you'll love.

CHAPTER TWO

The "Follow Your Passion" Hoax

I f there's one thing I've learned from talking with recent grads about their post-college job searches, it's that those who are the most frustrated—even panicked—are those who can't answer this question:

What type of job do I really want?

Until you can answer this, the odds of landing a good job are seriously stacked against you.

"But," you say, "I *really* don't know what I want to do!"

You're not alone. This uncertainty is part of being a young adult. In fact, it's part of being an adult at any age in today's work world. Lots of your parents' friends continue to struggle with this question of what kind of work they'd really love to do.

You've been asked, "What do you want to be when you grow up?" since you were little. You used to be able to throw out any answer and everybody laughed or smiled approvingly: Captain America, a ballet dancer, a doctor, Justin Bieber. Now that question is much more serious because to go into the job market you must have a plausible answer.

How to Find Your Path

The next two chapters will help you answer the "What-do-I-want-to-do?" question. (Skip to Chapter 5 if you already have your answer.)

Maybe you have no clue yet what kind of job you want. Or you may have some strong ideas but limited knowledge of the actual job market in those areas. Wherever you are is okay. Unfortunately, it often doesn't feel that way, recalls Olivia, a Georgetown University psychology major:

> *Senior year I had no idea what I wanted to do, but I was surrounded by people who did. I had friends going for interviews with banks, consulting companies, and law firms. Some had job offers before Christmas. That just fed my anxiety. The whole thing was overwhelming.*

When it comes to getting a good job, you make it much harder on yourself if you don't develop some clarity about the type of work you want to do. But don't get hung up on trying to figure out your whole career or life plan. You just need to clearly identify your interests and passions so your story makes sense to others. You've got to convince potential employers that you know what you want to do, and that their job makes sense for you. And you need to have this spiel down, even if you don't believe it 100%.

Remember writing those essays for your college applications? "Why do you want to attend Highly Selective U.?" You had to come up with answers, even if you weren't totally convinced this was the school for you. It's the same deal when you're selling yourself for a job.

For example, you might tell people you're looking for:

- A marketing position with a small high-tech firm that uses my writing and social media skills, and takes advantage of my fluency in Spanish.

- An entry-level sales job in financial services where I can use my communication and analytic skills to improve performance.

- A position in administrative support in a nonprofit organization where I can apply my excellent organizational and problem-solving skills.

I could write a whole book on how to figure out what kind of job you want, but I'm pretty sure you wouldn't read it. (See "Other Resources For Focusing Your Search.") So here's a short course on how to start solving this dilemma. What steps you take depends on how focused you are now.

Other Resources for Focusing Your Search

There are several good books that can help you discover what kind of work you might thrive on. Here are some of the best:

- *What Color is Your Parachute? 2013 A Practical Manual for Job-Hunters and Career Changers* by Richard Bolles, Ten Speed Press, 2012. This is a classic, and it's updated regularly to reflect the changing job market. You can't go wrong with this book. Tons of exercises and practical advice.

- *You Majored in What? Mapping Your Path From Chaos to Career* by Katherine Brooks, Plume, 2010.
  This book is ideal for liberal arts majors who are trying to translate their degrees into a successful job search. Lots of creative exercises.

- *The Pathfinder: How to Choose or Change Your Career...etc, etc.* by Nicholas Lore, Touchstone Books, 2012.
  This is a solid, very helpful book, but don't buy it unless you are prepared to do some serious thinking about yourself and your career. It is text and exercise heavy, but your investment could be well worth it.

- *Do What You Are: Discover the Perfect Career For You Through the Secrets of Personality Type* by Paul Tieger and Barbara Barron-Tieger, Little-Brown, 2007.
  Great for Myers-Briggs Personality Type fanatics. It's lighter going but will give you lots of insights into jobs that are more likely to fit your personality.

The Fallacy of "Following Your Passion"

One of the biggest dilemmas facing most new grads is how to find work they really enjoy that will also pay the bills. There is a strong push in career planning circles (maybe your parents promote it) to encourage grads to "find your passion" or "do what makes you happy." There are a couple of problems with this advice. One is described by an economics and English literature double major from Trinity College who says:

> When it comes to my career, my parents have let me be. But right now I have one arrow and I'm looking at ten different targets. As nice as it is to hear "We just want you to be happy," it's just a little too vague.

In 2005, Steve Jobs, the late founder of Apple, delivered a now-famous commencement speech at Stanford University encouraging students to find out what they're passionate about and then pursue work to match it. His powerful message was widely quoted. Unfortunately, this turns out to be terrible career advice, says Cal Newport, author of a terrific book, *So Good They Can't Ignore You: Why Skills Trump Passion in the Quest for Work You Love.*

Indeed, if Jobs himself had followed his own advice in his twenties, he would have ended up a teacher at an uber-funky Zen Center in Oregon, and you'd have never heard of the iPhone.

"Follow your passion" is extremely popular career advice, but it usually doesn't work for young grads. Research, according to Newport, consistently shows that people with successful careers rarely know what work they love until they try something and get really good at it. There are exceptions, of course. There were two grads out of my 30-plus case studies who knew what they were passionate about throughout college and then got jobs in their fields. The rest had to figure it out along the way.

The next time someone encourages you to "follow your passion," ask to hear the gory details about how this person's career started right after college. Chances are they knocked around in a few jobs before discovering work they liked and that was financially sustainable. So stop beating yourself up.

Instead of trying to figure out your calling, follow these principles when trying to focus your post-college job search:

Seek out work opportunities where you can develop valuable skills. Building capabilities that employers value, such as sales or project management skills, or knowledge about using new technologies, is much more likely to lead to more appealing jobs in the future. Marco's post-grad internship at Disney gave him a chance to acquire valuable website management skills making him a prime candidate for a great marketing position. (See the "Special Section: Search Strategies That Paid Off" for more of Marco's story.) When exploring different opportunities ask questions about the skills you can acquire if you really stretch yourself in the job.

Look for work situations that are likely to create "open gates" to new opportunities. Landing a job where you can acquire useful skills is hard, but once you gain momentum and an inside track, says Newport, it's much easier to shift roles or even organizations. If you are in a related job, employers are more likely to see a new role as a logical extension of what you've been doing. For example, Ethan took a position as an administrator for a struggling nonprofit only to find himself catapulted into a job as assistant director when the agency went through a major reorganization a few months after he arrived. It's a job he'd never be hired for from the outside. When looking at your options, favor organizations that are growing or likely to be going through changes, which could create opportunities for you to take on new challenges.

Recognize that there are multiple paths that if pursued enthusiastically will evolve into a career you love. In *So Good They Can't Ignore You*, Newport says stop worrying about "which path forward is your true calling." The key, once you get an opportunity, is to concentrate on distinguishing yourself by developing skills that are unique and valuable. But to find jobs where working your butt off will reward you with invaluable skills, Newport recommends avoiding three types of situations:

- Positions that offer little chance of developing capabilities that future employers would really value. For example, jobs as an insurance underwriter, call-center operator, and retail clerk come to mind.

- Jobs you consider useless or even bad for society. You need to engage with the work emotionally to standout.

- Situations in which you're forced to work with people you actively dislike.

Avoid these scenarios, and you can be wildly successful starting out in a wide variety of jobs after college. Focusing your job search so you will find work you love is not about landing the *perfect* job. It depends much more on what you do once you get a job.

"How I Figured Out What I Wanted to Do"

The last section of this book includes detailed stories of how some recent grads decided what they wanted to do and the kinds of jobs they pursued after school. These accounts show how decisions about work evolve over time, largely through trial and error. In Chapter 4 you also may be reassured by the experiences of two other new grads who struggled to find their focus. Lily, who graduated from University of California, Santa Barbara with an art history degree, ended up with an Internet marketing job. Tyler, on the other hand, got a communications degree from Louisiana State University and took a position as an executive recruiter. Here are some important insights from Lily and Tyler's experiences.

Lessons From Recent Grads

Cool-looking careers can quickly lose appeal when the realities of the job become evident. You may still be intent on pursuing your passion, whether it's art, film, journalism, or working for a nonprofit. Knock yourself out! But you also need to recognize the realities of what it actually means to work in the field you're targeting, and the sacrifices you'll have to make to succeed. Through internships in art galleries, Lily learned that "working in art" was a lot different and less appealing than "studying art." Tyler discovered being a TV reporter meant moving to a small town for a salary that wouldn't even cover his college loans.

A director of career services at one major university says:

I tell students you can't be a social worker, drive an expensive car, live in a big house, and go on exotic vacations unless you marry well, have a trust fund or hit the lottery. Social work just doesn't pay that well and never will.

Don't get hung up about not having a lifelong career plan. Most longer-term career interests only come into focus after working several years. Even then, experts predict you will have several different careers in the next 40 years. For now, try finding a job that will give you experiences so you can discover what you like and don't like about different types of work. Lily's research, for example, convinced her she had a strong desire to pursue marketing in a small-company environment. So she started going after those jobs with a lot more confidence.

What Kind of Job Will You Land?

There are five types of jobs you can end up in after college. Which one are you headed for?

Genuinely "Great Job"—Luke is working as a bank examiner for the Federal Reserve Bank and Faith is a graphic designer in a small firm. Both absolutely love what they're doing and whom they are doing it with. They can't see themselves anywhere else—right now! Less than 10% will land jobs like this right after college.

"Good Job"—Pablo is in financial sales, Olivia is a marketing coordinator and Ethan is an associate director of a nonprofit. These recent grads like what they are doing. They're learning a lot and working with good people. But they know they will probably be doing something different in a few years. This is where most "successful" college grads end up—if they're lucky. You're in a job that's a good learning experience, pays okay, and is a stepping-stone to something else.

"Temp Job"—This is a part-time job or temporary position in a field you might want to work in, but it's not a permanent position. Marco's post-college paid internship at Disney is an example. So is Andrew's stint as a substitute teacher. These jobs can be a useful springboard, but the pressure is always on to convert this assignment into something more long term.

"Treading Water Job"—These are jobs you might take after graduating just to pay the rent. Sometimes it's called being "fun-employed," which is definitely better than unemployed. Dirk was a bartender in Washington, D.C., while looking for a job in journalism. Sara waitressed in a Chicago restaurant while trying to break into the nonprofit world. These jobs might even pay pretty well for now, *but they are definitely not what you went* *to college to do.* It's a good alternative to not having a job, but you won't be bragging about this work at your college reunion.

"Bad Job"—Among those who appeared to be successfully employed after graduating, about 10% ended up in really toxic jobs. A job is not "bad" because you have to work too hard, or even because the pay is low. It's unbearable because your boss or co-workers are totally screwed up or the organization's values seriously contradict your own. Tyler was hired by a recruiting firm where he was encouraged to lie to clients to do his job. He began looking for a new job immediately. Andrew's first job in a small New York nonprofit had him working for a callous boss that left him visibly depressed and losing weight.

If you want to avoid ending up in a "Treading Water Job," or if you're in one now and desperately want to get out, the best way to start is by focusing your job search using the resources described in Chapter 3.

Be prepared to demonstrate knowledge related to jobs you want. Just being smart, willing to work hard and learn doesn't really cut it with companies today. Lily discovered this the hard way, when she told potential employers she wanted any position where she could work hard and learn. She applied for almost 200 jobs but got only a handful of unsuccessful interviews using this approach. To become successful, Lily poured over marketing websites and technology blogs to learn the jargon and the issues relevant to those marketing jobs for which she might land an interview.

Watch out when financial obligations or big paychecks take priority over your other values. Sometimes it feels absolutely necessary to pursue a job for the money. But plenty of people take jobs for big salaries and end up hating them. Have you done enough research actually talking to people to get a *real* feel for what it would be like to work as a financial analyst or a pharmaceutical rep? You may decide to pursue a field where you know you're going to work killer hours, but you'll also make gobs of money. Go for it! Just check out the values and priorities of the people you'll be working with. Tyler jumped into the recruiting business without realizing it would force him to compromise his values in ways he couldn't accept. He couldn't get out of that job fast enough!

Don't underestimate the value of adding "practical" courses to your resume. This is true if you're a first-year college student or you've already graduated. Lily added a professional writing minor senior year that gave her experience writing for the Web. This ended up being directly related to her first job. Tyler took an "Introduction to public relations" class senior year with a professor who would be key in refocusing his career. Carl graduated with an economics degree from Colorado College but found that potential employers in investment management weren't impressed. So, while looking for a job, he began studying for the Chartered Financial Analyst designation. Passing several tests in this program made him much more marketable.

Don't panic if, like Lily or Tyler, you're feeling uncertain about what kind of work you want to do. You're like a lot of undergraduates or new college grads. And don't get paralyzed by the "follow your passion" hoax either. Your task now is to take action to get out of the starting gate. Narrow your focus and clarify your story, so you can land a job in a field that looks promising, where you can start developing skills that will open doors to other opportunities. The next chapter will show you how to speed up this process.

CHAPTER THREE

Three Ways to Focus Your Job Search

Which of these stories from new grads comes closest to describing your situation?

- *Tristan always believed there was more to college than just studying. And, as he prepared to graduate from American University with a degree in environmental science, he didn't know what he wanted to do. "When thinking about life after college, I wasn't stressing," he recalls. "I had a girlfriend. I was chillin', hanging out. I had so much success with my internship, I figured I'd get a job no problem."*

- *Andrew graduated from Bowdoin College with a double major in English and theater. Originally interested in sports marketing, a couple of internships convinced Andrew he wanted to be in New York City working in marketing, PR, or maybe advertising. Being in New York, he also could keep his dreams of acting in the theater alive.*

- *Zoey finished her undergraduate degree at Central Michigan University as a recreation major. (Okay, it's not what you think! This is a serious discipline.) Since sophomore year, she had become extremely interested in event planning. All her internships and extracurricular activities were focused on getting experience in the hospitality and event-planning industry. Zoey knew the types of jobs she wanted to pursue when she graduated and she'd learned a lot about the industry while in college.*

Are you Tristan, Andrew, or Zoey? There's no right answer. The key is telling yourself the truth about your starting point because that will help determine where you need to spend your time. Maybe you're one of the lucky ones, like Zoey, who by senior year knew exactly what she wanted to do. (If so, skip to Chapter 5.) Or maybe you're like Tristan and have no clue what kind of job you want. Or you could have some strong ideas, like Andrew, but limited knowledge of the actual job market in those areas.

It's okay *not* to know what you want to do. But it's not okay to do nothing to clarify your work interests and passions. Here are a few things you can start doing immediately to determine what kinds of jobs you want to go after. Remember, the goal isn't to plan the rest of your life. You're just trying to find work situations, jobs, and companies that fit your current interests and needs. Combining resources from your career center, informational interviews, and online research is a great way to bring your job search into focus. It also will make your parents much more bearable around the holidays!

Exploit Career Services for All It's Worth

One recent study found that students who proactively used career-counseling resources at their school increased their median starting salary by more than $5,700 over those who never used the services. Even if you have already graduated, this center can be an important resource for figuring out what you want to do. Career services offices today are under a lot of pressure to help deliver a payoff for that expensive degree you've invested in.

Of course, some university career centers are much better than others. If you're lucky, yours will have experienced counselors to help you think creatively about work options that make sense for you. They'll also have diagnostic tests you can take to get feedback on your strengths and weaknesses to identify careers and jobs that should be more engaging. When you start this process, having realistic expectations will reduce the panic factor. None of the successful grads interviewed ever said, "I knew exactly what I wanted to do when I left career services." Figuring out what you want to do for work is a journey. It's not a problem a career counselor will solve for you in an hour or two.

The Pros & Cons of Career Tests*

Olivia was a Georgetown University psychology major who ended up working in marketing and PR for a software company. She remembers taking tests when trying to get clearer career direction.

I took a bunch of tests online, such as Myers-Briggs. I was hoping I could just take one where you press a button and the next screen says, "Here is your career path," but it's not that simple! You take the tests online and the results say, "You are 30 percent like people who are veterinarians."

Tests can provide you with important insights about yourself, but they can't reliably predict what kind of job is best for you. Career-related tests will tell you if your responses match people who do particular types of jobs. But they can't tell you if you have the capabilities or right degrees to be a teacher, investment banker, or sales person.

Still there are some tests that will give you more self-knowledge to help you describe yourself in interviews. These results also can reinforce your own intuition about your strengths and weaknesses. If getting another perspective on your strengths and aptitudes is appealing, skip the horoscope and Tarot-card readings, and find out if your career center offers these tests:

- Campbell Interest and Skills Survey
- Myers-Briggs Type Indicator
- Strong Interest Inventory

You also can take these tests on your own:

- Buy the book *Now, Discover Your Strengths* by Marcus Buckingham and Donald O. Clifton. It gives you a code to take their cool "Strengths Inventory" online.

- Check out the Authentic Happiness website at www.AuthenticHappiness.sas.upenn.edu/ to take the "Values in Action" (VIA) test

*Adapted from *You Majored in What? Mapping Your Path From Chaos to Career* by Katherine Brooks, New York: Plume, 2009.

It's Never Too Soon to Start Doing "Informational Interviews"!

Maybe you've heard this term and you're rolling your eyes or maybe it's a new concept to you. Either way, these interviews are probably your most powerful tool for learning what you want to do for work. Here's how Ryan, a finance grad from Fordham University, used these conversations to clarify his thinking about what he wanted to do.

I had become more interested in picking stocks, taking a more active role in financial investing, what they call "the buy side." A friend of my father's put me in touch with some people in the business, and we talked by phone about how the investing process had changed in the industry. At that point, I was trying to figure out if I wanted to work on the buy side, and what sort of experience I needed to get.

I also had a friend a year ahead of me in school who worked at Citigroup's investment bank. He had a typical Wall Street job, working 90 hours a week. It was really stressful. We met for lunch and he'd lost 25 pounds. He offered me a lot of advice on going through the investment job-search process. But you can't rely on one person's advice. So I talked to any other sources I could find. My Dad put me in touch with a guy running a commodities consulting firm in New York who had unique insights about industry hiring trends.

There's a lot more about informational interviews in Chapter 12 because the people who get good jobs use them very successfully. If you're a confirmed introvert and the thought of having these face-to-face conversations scares the hell out of you, read "Networking for Introverts" in Chapter 12. In the meantime, here are two things you need to know to start using this approach today:

Never Ask For A Job. These conversations are low risk because you are asking for something everybody can give you—the story of their career so far and advice based on their experience. You are not asking for a job. This is very important. Probably 99.5% of the time, people don't have a job to give you, anyway. So, if you ask them for one or where to find one, they have to turn you down. If you ask people for something they can't give you, they feel bad. But ask for something they can easily give you—advice—and they feel great if they think it's helping.

Prepare Questions. Always go into an informational interview with questions to get the other person talking about their work, their experiences and any advice they can offer you about getting started in a particular type of business. (So when did you know you wanted to be a lion tamer? Does the career path for an astronaut follow a typical trajectory?) You can develop your own questions based on what you're trying to learn at this early stage of your job search. Here are six questions to get you started:

- How did you get into <u>investment banking</u>?

- What do you like most/least about your work as a <u>swordfish boat captain</u>?

- How do people get started in <u>nuclear reactor operations</u>? What are the entry-level possibilities for someone like me?

- What would you do if you were in my shoes trying to find work in <u>journalism</u> today?

- Can you think of two or three other people I might speak with to learn more about becoming a <u>concert promoter</u>?

- May I use your name when I contact them?

Informational interviews play a different role when your job search becomes more focused. (I'll describe this in more detail in Chapter 12.) These conversations are essential for making sense of all the other information you will collect at your career center and in your Web research.

Three Keys to Using the Internet for Effective Career Planning

The current job market may look lousy, but the irony is young people graduating from college today have more career choices than any previous generation. Not only are there more types of jobs out there, but now more information than ever is available about specific roles, thanks to the Internet. This combination of more job options and more information about them can be overwhelming to a student or recent graduate trying to explore what work opportunities they should pursue. Do follow these three steps and you'll make your research phase more efficient and helpful.

1. Keep your options open during your initial research. Obviously, if you already feel strongly about the type of work you want, it is much easier to decide what jobs to research. Career experts like Lindsey Pollak warn against closing in too fast on what you want to do. In *Getting from College to Career*, Pollak advises creating a "Really Big List" of every career possibility of interest to you. The idea at this stage is to stay open to as many options as possible. This type of divergent thinking will help you be more successful in the long run. Manny Contomanolis heads career services at Rochester Institute of Technology. He explains:

> *There are kids who come into our office and announce they want to be an investment banker and will only talk to these six firms. And then there are others who only want to work for Microsoft, Google, or Facebook. Students who are more flexible and realistic about what they want to do are more successful in job searches today.*

2. Focus Internet searches through career-related gateway websites. Just start searching the Web helter-skelter for ideas about jobs and you'll quickly be overwhelmed with tons of marginally relevant and questionably accurate information. You're much better off going to large Web portals organized for job seekers by experts who have reviewed the content listed. Check out these portals to begin your career research:

A. http://www.job-hunt.org/job-search-for-new-grads/
   job-search-for-new-grads.shtml
   A very cool, focused site to help you start thinking about your career.

B. http://www.rileyguide.com/careers.html
Well-respected site with links to hundreds of articles
and reports to expand your ideas about career options.

C. http://dsc.discovery.com/tv/dirty-jobs/
For opportunities where there just isn't much competition,
visit this website for "Dirty Jobs," the Discovery Channel
show that celebrates hard work in the most trying settings.
Learn about career opportunities in exotic jobs, such as
shark-suit tester, avian vomitologist, sheep castrator, sewer
inspector, and medical-waste disposal. Not interested?
Who do you think is going to do these jobs in the future?

D. http://www.quintcareers.com/career_exploration.html
A more serious set of career-exploration tools and resources.
Includes a great annotated list of links to resources you
can use.

E. http://careerplanning.about.com/od/exploringoccupations/
a/exploration.htm
Watch out for the ads, but this About.com site is another
good place to start exploring career options.

F. http://www.ceoexpress.com/asp/bp.asp
CEOExpress is a cool site for finding and tracking business-
related links fast. This link takes you to its detailed listing
of industries/fields to explore. I use CEOExpress.com as
my highly customizable home page.

G. http://www.payscale.com/research/US/Country=United_
States/Salary
When you have a specific job in mind, this is a good place
to check out what you might expect to be paid. Your
parents will probably be visiting this site when they learn
what jobs you're thinking about.

Your school's career center also will have plenty of online resources that should be helpful in your preliminary research. If you can't immediately figure out what's useful, call or visit them and ask for advice on where to find what you need.

3. Spell out immediate research goals and limit your screen time. It's easy to get overwhelmed by the volume of information on the Internet. So write down your goals and intentions before you start browsing, even if you're using the well-organized sites listed previously. For example, say, "In the next hour, I'm going to learn whatever I can about entry-level marketing jobs in nonprofit organizations." Or "I'm going to do a twenty-minute search for articles on what it takes to be a financial advisor to see if that sounds interesting."

Having a specific reason for your search and setting a time limit will keep you from getting lost, mired, and distracted by all the irrelevant but "interesting" things you will stumble upon while doing research.

Brooke, a sociology major graduating from University of California, Berkeley, read a lot of postings for different types of jobs on Craigslist.org when trying to figure out what she wanted to do after graduation. "I kept asking myself, 'Does this sound like something I'd like to do?'" she says. Then she would check out sites like PayScale.com and Glassdoor.com that give salary ranges for jobs she found interesting. Social work was a field Brooke initially considered. But her interest faded when she learned there were plenty of jobs requiring only a bachelor's degree that paid more than social work positions, which almost always require a master's degree. As she continued her research, Brooke also felt less stress when she lowered the stakes on the question she was trying to answer.

I became less focused on finding my future career path and more on what is something that will give me good experience and create transferable skills. I just wanted to find something interesting in the short term, which I was qualified to do.

To improve your odds of short-term success in the job market, start using informational interviews, input from your career services office, and Web research to get more specific ideas of what you want to do. Taking these steps also will give you insights into your competition and how the hiring game is played in fields you want to pursue. But to have realistic expectations about whether you can land the job you want, you need to have a good idea of how potential employers will evaluate you. That's the focus of Chapter 5. In the meantime, Chapter 4 shows how two recent grads—Lily and Tyler—made decisions that got them their first jobs after school.

Checklist for Action:
Decide What You're Looking For

Students and recent grads travel very different paths when figuring out what kind of jobs they want. And it's okay not to have an answer right now. But what's your starting point? Are you clueless or do you have some pretty clear ideas? Regardless, stop trying to figure out your *entire* career. It's going to change anyway. In the meantime, here are five things you can do now to make progress on this question of what job you want.

___1. **Make an appointment at your school's career services office.** Have you asked around to see if any classmates can recommend a particularly helpful career counselor there? Just because your immediate friends aren't using the career office doesn't mean you shouldn't check it out. These people are being paid to help you succeed *after* college!

___2. **Ask a career counselor about useful career tests to take.**

___3. **Set a goal to conduct two informational interviews per month if you're an underclassman, more if you're a senior or a graduate.** If you're on campus, you can pursue professors, local companies, or interview your roommates' parents by phone. Just get started!

___4. **Once you have particular careers or fields in mind, do more research.** Learn about typical career paths and the realities of working in the field day to day. Combining Web research and informational interviews will accelerate your learning and build confidence.

____5. Consider practical electives or training outside of school that will make you a stronger candidate in the fields you are considering.

CHAPTER FOUR

How Two Grads Found Their First Jobs

I n researching this book, I interviewed more than 30 recent grads who landed excellent jobs. Their stories are all different, but the tactics they used and the emotions they experienced along the way are remarkably similar.

Here are two of those stories. Even if their journeys don't fit your specific situation, you can learn valuable lessons from their experiences.

Skip this chapter for now if your focus is on taking immediate action. But I invite you to come back to it when you're feeling anxious or frustrated. These are real stories from people who were standing in your shoes. They encountered the same lows and highs that define job searches today and came out winners. You can, too.

For more inspiring examples of how students and recent grads made the most of internships, networking, job-search technologies, and interviews see the Special Section: Search Strategies That Paid Off.

Lily, University of California, Santa Barbara:
From Art History to Internet Marketing

Like many recent grads, Lily didn't have a clear idea what she wanted to do, and her initial plan became even less appealing over time. She explains how she turned things around.

Sophomore year, I became an art history major because I enjoyed the classes. I spent fall semester junior year studying in Rome, which left me even more excited about working in art. I had a romantic idea of working in a huge museum in a big city. That summer I took internships in two galleries and learned that studying art was not the same as working in art. Art is just a retail business. It is not about curating fun collections. I also talked with students who got jobs in museums and all they did was write grants to raise money. It was a sobering experience.

Senior year, I was suddenly terrified of not being in college anymore. I had a group of friends who felt the same way. We weren't going to look at our work options until we graduated. So I did the most practical thing I could think of and signed up for a minor in multimedia and professional writing. I learned Photoshop, HTML, and writing for the Web.

I moved home to the Bay Area after graduation and started applying for jobs with no focus except to work at a place that was young and fun. I just told companies I wanted to work hard and learn, and I expected to get a job pretty quickly. But, I got no response 99 percent of the time when I applied for jobs.

My Dad who has 25 years experience working with tech startups helped me get informational interviews that made all the difference. People I spoke with convinced me I had to hone my skills. If I was interested in marketing, I had to learn about brands, and to learn about brands I had to be reading the right blogs, such as TechCrunch. So I began doing that every day.

By late August, I was learning the lingo and sounded more qualified than I felt. I was feeling better because I started getting more responses to my applications. In November, I landed a job with a small, Web-based education company. Truthfully, I didn't understand what an "ad operations coordinator" was when I took it. But because it's a start up, I'm doing different things every day, and I'm always learning.

Tyler, Louisiana State University:
Communications Major Takes a Lucrative Turn Into the Wrong Job

Even when you have identified a field you're determined to work in, your career path may take you to unexpected places. How do you make the right decision, especially when income is a deciding factor? Here's the story of how Tyler's career began to unfold when he took a job primarily for money. See "Happy Endings" in Chapter 20 to learn the rest of his story.

My father had died when I was 16. So when I started college, I wanted to do whatever I could to bring in the most money. At first, I went into accounting, but I hated the classes. When Hurricane Katrina hit New Orleans, it displaced my family, and I left school for a while. I worked for almost a year as a production assistant at the Fox TV affiliate in New Orleans. A producer took me under his wing and encouraged me to write a little broadcast news.

I returned to college at Louisiana State and auditioned for a position as an anchor on Tiger TV, the student run TV station. I got the job and junior year I worked as a reporter and a news producer.

Junior year I also took my first print writing class because it was required. Print wasn't my thing, but I got the best grades in the class. The professor worked for a local paper and offered me a job as a part-time reporter. Then senior year, I added a class in public relations. The professor made PR really fun.

By senior year, I was website director at the TV station, and creating video packages in my spare time so I could submit them when applying for jobs. I realized I would have to send tapes to TV stations all over the country and, if I was lucky, I'd get picked up in a small town. Also, I had $30,000 in student loans and I knew I might not be able to pay them with the salary in my first job as a TV reporter. I had a lot of anxiety approaching graduation.

I had always been a big Disney fan, and I learned they had an internship opening in Orlando. My PR professor encouraged me to apply and I was offered the position. I wanted to get out of Louisiana, and it paid more than an entry-level job in TV. At Disney, I found I really enjoyed being on the other side of the media, being in PR instead of a reporter. Still, I had only solved my problem of what I was going to do for that year. When my internship at Disney ended, there were no staff positions available. I got really, really nervous about what to do next.

I was lying in bed one night and a LinkedIn message popped up from a recruiting firm. I thought it was spam at first, but I did some research and decided to talk to them. They were looking for an entry-level recruiter. There was nothing really that excited me about the job, but they offered me $50,000, which was a lot more than I had been making. I took the money, but in less than a month, I knew I had made a mistake. I was taught to lie to get executives on the phone, but I'm not that kind of salesman. If I did well, I could make an ungodly amount of money, like my bosses, but it was not worth who I had to become. I had to get the hell out.

See Chapter 20 for the rest of Tyler's story. No matter how you decide what job you want to pursue, you're going to have to compete with others for the position. Chapter 5 helps you stack the odds in your favor.

CHAPTER FIVE

How Will You Stack Up Against the Competition?

I t's one thing to have your career interests come into focus and to know what kinds of jobs you want to pursue. But before you even get to an interview, you also have to understand how you will be seen as a job applicant.

- How will employers view your resume and track record compared to other applicants?

- Are there standard hiring processes or rules of thumb you need to know about your target industry or employer so you will be taken seriously?

- What is the competition like for the jobs you're interested in? There's a rivalry for every hot job, of course, but for fields like finance, video-game design, and entertainment the number of people trying to get jobs is crazy!

Answer these questions as you consider the fields, types of jobs, or companies for which you want to work. They will help you set realistic expectations about where you can be successful in your job search.

How to Set Realistic Expectations

Do I have the degrees or majors that make me a viable candidate for this type of work? As a rule, employers don't hire based on majors, but a religious studies major applying for a bank job is probably at a disadvantage, just as a math major would be in applying for a journalism job.

Is a potential employer going to see any evidence on my resume that I have shown an interest in this career area? That is, relevant internships, volunteer experiences, courses, memberships. You may be able to explain this away when you get into an interview. However, if you are approaching a big company with lots of applicants, it's unlikely you'll get through the initial screening process if your resume doesn't suggest interests pertinent to the job.

Are there gaps in my resume I still have time to fill? For example, if you've recently decided you're interested in international business, but have done nothing abroad, could you take an offshore elective over winter break? Or, if you have already graduated, is there a technology course or certification you want to go for to make you a more attractive candidate in a particular field? Maybe you'll need to take on a post-graduation internship because you just don't have enough experience in the industry you're targeting. Before investing your time and money in things to supplement your resume do get advice from someone who knows the field to make sure your investment will be worth it.

Is the job I'm shooting for realistic, given my level of experience? Sure you may have had three great internships, but the job description says, "5 years of experience required." It's one thing to consider jobs asking for 1-2 years of experience, but don't waste your time applying for jobs you *clearly* aren't qualified to do.

Increase the Role of Luck in Your Job Search

Hoping that good luck will help you launch your career is a terrible job-search strategy. Failing to understand the rules of the game and how the odds are stacked against you invites a long-term stay on your parents' couch.

You may be graduating from Stanford University with a fantastic GPA, a string of great internships, a clear career focus, and a killer network of contacts eager to help you. Or you could be finishing your degree with a lousy GPA from the local community college with no internship experiences because you had to work extra shifts at Starbucks to pay your way through school. Guess who will get "luckier" landing a good job? Obviously, the odds are stacked in favor of the Stanford grad. But here are three things you can do to influence the role luck plays in your job search, once you know the real odds of the game you're playing.

1. Focus on creating a good job-search process. In situations where you can't predict or control the outcomes, like in a job search, the best way to improve your odds is to focus on creating a better process. This includes networking and using technology effectively, creating a killer resume, and improving your interviewing skills.

2. Create opportunities for "lucky" events. Unplanned events will inevitably shape your career. To change your luck, put yourself in more social situations where good things can happen. Then be ready to take advantage of them. Madison accompanied her aunt to a meeting with a prominent doctor and ended up with a research internship that led to a job. Dirk met a prominent political consultant at a cocktail party who became a key mentor. Molly accompanied her brother to a job fair and ended up with an offer herself.

3. Watch for key incremental changes that could make a big difference. Sometimes adding one practical, skill-building course can be a "tipping point" in making you a much stronger job candidate. Lily added a professional writing minor senior year, which proved critical to landing her first job. Scoring a part-time job in your school's career center also can be a game changer. Becoming more fluent in a second language is another relatively small decision that could dramatically change your luck during your job search.

So how will you generate luck? Focus on creating and maintaining a good search process, instead of getting hung up on each job you don't get. Then create opportunities for lucky events to happen, and watch for small changes that could make you a stronger candidate.

Learn the Rules of the Game You're Playing

Even if you have the grades and the extracurricular activities to make you a viable candidate, you need to understand the expectations of the field or company you are trying to approach. Do they have a particular hiring season? Does the company hire *only* from targeted schools? What role do internships play in its hiring process?

While at Colorado College, Carl decided he wanted to work in investment banking, but he was unprepared for a job search in this field.

After my junior year, I went to New York and got an internship in a week through my father's contacts. That gave me the wrong impression of how hard it would be to find a job the following year. I thought I was on the fast track to finding a sweet invest-ment-banking job or working at a hedge fund. But I didn't think about how my course work related to the outside world and my job search. My major in economics didn't give me specific know-how for the investment field I wanted to get into. Senior year I did some interviews in December, but I had missed the boat for recruiting at the larger banks. I didn't realize they did their hiring earlier in the fall.

Andrew, a Bowdoin College grad, searched for jobs in advertising after his first post-college job proved to be a disaster.

I discovered advertising was very competitive to break into. Big ad agencies typically hire only from within their intern program or through internal connections. Also, people in the business said it was easier to get in on the account management side. But I was only interested in the creative side of advertising. The business was very hard to break into and I had no connections.

Of course you will hear occasional stories of how a classmate landed a plum job in a cool firm when it looked like she had no chance. These people are the lucky exceptions. Hoping to get lucky is fine for dating, but it's a terrible job-search strategy.

This isn't American Idol: How to Stack the Odds in Your Favor

Just because your class rank is nothing to brag about and you don't have cool internship experiences to flaunt doesn't mean there isn't a great job out there for you. There is! You just aren't going to find it at a name-brand company like Google, Goldman Sachs, Proctor & Gamble, MTV, or Disney. You might as well go buy another lottery ticket.

I'm not trying to bum you out. It's just that the job market is so competitive these days that unless you're a rock-star student, with lots of related work or internship experiences, you're wasting your time applying to high-profile companies with huge applicant pools, unless you have an inside connection. (See Chapter 10.) There are still plenty of great organizations and awesome jobs out there.

To stack the odds in your favor, think of this process just like when you were applying to colleges. Sometime in high school you probably got the idea that your chances of getting into Duke, Caltech, or Yale were slim. Now you need to do some realistic benchmarking about where your job applications will put you in a strong competitive position. Unfortunately, your transcript and lack of experience is going to take you out of the running for certain high-profile jobs. However, that doesn't mean hard work, some smart career moves and a little luck won't catapult you to success beyond your wildest dreams!

Part of understanding how you stack up against the competition is recognizing the value of the internships and other work experiences you have on your resume. How do you make good decisions about internships before—and after—graduation? How do you maximize the value of these experiences to shorten your job search? That's what you'll learn in the next few chapters.

Checklist for Action:
Assess Your Employability

To be seriously considered for more jobs, you need to get a realistic assessment of how potential employers will see you. Of course, everything is relative. You may be a lousy candidate for a high-profile investment banking job in New York, but a terrific candidate for a financial analyst job with a small company in Omaha. Collect feedback from a variety of sources.

____1. **Ask a counselor in career services to evaluate your strengths and weaknesses as a candidate for particular jobs.** The quality of this feedback, of course, depends on the counselor's experience and knowledge of fields you're interested in. Use your judgment, but be a little skeptical of the advice you get.

____2. **When you do informational interviews with people who have *current* knowledge of industries or types of jobs you're interested in, always ask them to critique your resume.** Ask what you can do to make yourself a stronger candidate.

____3. **Ask for feedback from recruiters who visit your campus during job fairs about the strengths and weaknesses they see in your resume.** You have to pick the right times to do this. Don't just walk up to someone and ask for feedback. Once you've connected with a recruiter, learned about the company, and if he or she seems interested in talking, then you might ask for guidance.

_____4. Look for postings of the jobs you might apply for and evaluate how many key words in the job description also appear in your resume. If the answer is "not many," then either revise your resume (see Chapter 15) or pursue other opportunities.

CHAPTER SIX

Why Internships Have Changed the Game

Experience. It's the first thing employers are looking for in a job candidate, and it's the one thing you probably don't have!

If you're an underclassman, you'll find out soon enough that employers want candidates who can hit the ground running. And if you've been looking for a job, you've already learned about this the hard way. In fact, you've heard the "I-word"—internship, that is—until you're sick of it. Like it or not, one of the most critical things in getting a great job is the experiences you've had and the skills you've demonstrated while spending time in organizations *before* graduation—or soon after.

In the next few chapters, you'll learn how successful recent grads are using internship experiences to separate themselves from the pack. You'll also find out how to:

- Decide what type of internship you want to pursue.

- Get valuable internships faster.

- Maximize the value of *post-grad* internships.

- Make sure internships pay off in your job search.

- Get other types of experiences that make you a stronger candidate.

What's the Difference Between an Internship and a Job?

There's all kinds of mumbo-jumbo written about what qualifies as an "internship" as opposed to a "job." For the purposes of our discussion, let's call an internship any opportunity to gain work-related experience in an organization where someone is supervising you, giving you useful direction about what you should be learning, and offering feedback on how well you're doing.

Whether or not your internship is for course credit, career counselors will advise you that these "experiential learning opportunities" need to include "intentional learning goals." In practice, however, the goals of internships are often vague at the outset. You may or may not find your classroom learning relevant. And you most certainly will be asked to do at least some routine work—data entry, filing, photocopying, etc. Frankly, getting this kind of work done may be the only reason some companies invite you in the first place.

Employers often use the word "internship" to describe a temporary job, which they can get a student to do for free, or for little pay. The trick, of course, is to find ways to balance getting the grunt work done, with finding opportunities to learn valuable, resume-building skills—such as updating the company website, doing research, or writing press releases. You can bitch about how companies use—and abuse—interns, or you can recognize the way the system works and use it to *your* advantage.

To find internships to build your experience base and your resume, look for positions that best suit your needs on three dimensions:

1. Length: how long do I have to do this?

Internships can last for a semester, a summer, or just a few weeks. Marco, for example, already had a communications degree from the University of Texas when he did a full-time, eight-month internship at Disney. Faith was a graphic design major at James Madison University when she interned for a big ad agency two days a week for six weeks during the summer. Don't overlook opportunities for short or part-time internships, particularly if the experience will expose you to a distinctly different type of organization or help you start to gain valuable new skills.

2. Exploratory or focused: why are you there?

Marco and Faith knew what kinds of jobs they wanted to land, so their internships focused on building skills and networks in specific fields. (See "Special Section: Search Strategies That Paid Off" to learn how Marco and Faith did this.) But what if you don't know what you want to do? Welcome to the club! At least half of the recent grads interviewed were in that situation while in school or after graduating. Internships and volunteer experiences can play a key role in helping you discover what you like and don't like in a work setting.

Katherine interned in the corporate offices of a major animal health products distributor after freshman year at the University of Texas. That was the summer she learned she hated sitting in a cubicle doing paperwork. Her next internship choice? A Web-based marketing role where she discovered she enjoyed interacting with people versus computer screens.

3. Paid vs. unpaid internships

Well-meaning employers and professional groups such as the National Association of Colleges and Employers (NACE) have spelled out criteria for when internships should be paid and unpaid. But many recent grads interviewed felt some companies were definitely pushing the boundaries of what should be a legitimate unpaid internship and what was slave labor. Still, of the scores of internships described in my interviews very few showed up as truly exploitive. Will you be asked to do some routine grunt work in an unpaid internship? Yes, probably. Will you still learn a ton if you keep your eyes open, ask lots questions, and make the most of your new contacts?

Most definitely. Will the experience you gain be more helpful in your quest for post-college employment than adding one more killer elective such as:

- "Zombies in Popular Media" (Columbia College Chicago)
- "How to Watch Television" (Montclair State University)
- "Maple Syrup: The Real Thing" (Alfred College)

You make the call. This isn't an argument against taking a fun class or two. Just recognize the choices you make in school may work against you later when you're in the job market.

The Pros & Cons of Post-Graduation Internships

Like it or not, there's a good chance you'll have to do something that will be labeled an "internship" *after* graduating from college. It may not seem fair, but some post-graduation internships are now substitutes for entry-level jobs. They can be a great way to break into an industry and to build your resume, despite killer hours and minimal pay. Or, as Ross Perlin points out in his provocative book *Intern Nation*, they can be thinly disguised slave labor with little hope of advancing your career. If possible, check out experiences other interns had at the company you are considering.

Laura, a Lehigh University journalism grad, was pleased to be working three days a week as an editorial intern at a glossy New York lifestyle magazine. (Meanwhile, her grandmother gave her pepper spray for the 4 a.m. walks home from her late-night job as a cocktail waitress.) This magazine internship seemed like a great resume builder until she realized the woman sitting next to her had been an intern there for five years!

Whether you think you can afford it or not, a low- or no-pay post-grad internship may be essential to get the experience you need to be competitive in today's job market. More than 30% of the "success story" job seekers interviewed chose to accept a post-graduate internship. About 50% of the people who chose to do these internships were paid a stipend, so they weren't working for free. In fact, some of these positions looked an awful lot like full-time jobs. Calling the position an "internship" meant employers weren't committed long term and didn't have to pay benefits.

Nobody said building a career would be fair…or fun for that matter. But this is the reality of trying to find work in highly competitive fields today.

"I Can't Afford an Internship"

The issue of unpaid—or low paid—internships is particularly difficult for students who must work to get through school and pay the bills immediately after graduation. Many undergrads can't afford to take an unpaid internship during the summer because they must make money to pay tuition and living expenses. The importance of internships for future employment definitely stacks the deck against students with limited financial resources, but there are some solutions.

If your financial resources are limited and unpaid internships are unfeasible, there are still things you can do to gain valuable experience:

—Structure part-time internships. Faith limited her internship with an ad agency to two days a week because she needed to earn money working in an upscale grocery store. Ultimately, hiring managers will be more interested in where you interned and what results you produced than how many hours per week you put in.

—Look for alternative funding sources. Don't overlook the possibility of getting a grant to fund your internship. Be sure to ask Career Services and the Internship Programs Office about opportunities for financial assistance. One University of Texas student scored an $8,000 grant from his school to spend the summer as an intern in New York City.

—*Don't underestimate the skills and values demonstrated in your paying jobs.* Maria had to pay her own tuition at Eastern Washington University where she was an education major. Not only did she work from 5 a.m. to 1 p.m. managing a coffee shop, she also took a job filing in a chiropractor's office starting at 10 p.m. In her spare time, she tutored struggling math students at her school. Her work ethic and the skills she acquired surely impressed potential employers, but Maria had to communicate this to those interviewing her.

—*Use your paying job to build your job-search network.* You never know what opportunities will come your way when people see you working hard to pursue your goal. When it's appropriate, be quick to tell your story to customers or adult co-workers. "I'm a student at the University where I'm studying...I'm working to pay tuition and I hope to work in...." Ethan, for example, got his first job at a local bank after graduating from Beloit College because he had met the bank's president while waiting tables at a local country club.

The concept of internships has changed a lot in recent years. The term is now used to describe *many* different situations where people are gaining work-related experience for little or no pay. The question is how can you use internships to maximize your value on the job market? The next chapter shows you how to land great internships faster.

Checklist for Action:
Decide Which Internship is Right For You

___1. **Are you still in the exploratory phase of your job search? Then what questions do you have about different jobs you might pursue?** What do these questions suggest about the types of internships that could be most helpful in getting answers? Industry, location, activities?

___2. **Make notes about what you've learned from the internships (and jobs) you had.** What aspects of the work and the environment did you really like and dislike? E.g., "I never want to work in a cubicle again." "I liked being part of a team in a small department."

___3. **If you're clear about the types of jobs you want, then examine current job postings and job descriptions to identify the skills you need to be a stronger candidate.** What types of internships will help you develop these skills?

___4. **If you're considering a post-grad internship, ask *other* potential employers about the pros and cons of doing this internship.** How will it make you a better job candidate?

___5. **If you can't afford to do an unpaid internship, explore creative options for getting more experience.** Make sure you're not overlooking opportunities for paid internships. Perhaps you can structure an internship for only a few hours a week to give you that valuable experience.

CHAPTER SEVEN

Get a Good Internship Faster–Before or After Graduation

"The fastest way to get an internship is to start early and pursue multiple opportunities diligently." *Are you kidding? Who listens to that advice?*

If you're a student, you're likely wondering how to land a great internship with as little effort as possible. Where do you find the most promising ones? And how do you decide which internship opportunities to accept or turn down? Read on for answers to these questions and more.

Of course, your career services office staff and your parents are right: it is better to start looking for internships early. But, even if you ignored that advice, where can you look?

Look in the Right Places at School

Helping students find great experiential learning opportunities is a big part of what colleges and universities do today. Of course, some do this better than others. Virtually all schools have internship databases and counselors to guide you through the search process. Of course, finding a good match depends on what kind of internship you're looking for and where you want to be geographically.

Zach, a history major at Colby College, recalls his experience trying to find an internship in Boston while studying in Europe.

It was fall, I was in the Czech Republic and I needed an internship in time for the January break, but I didn't know what I wanted to do. On the Colby careers website, students can search internships on a million criteria. I clicked anything that seemed remotely interesting that was located in Boston. Then I'd email people and just try to get in front of them by setting up a Skype call. That whole process taught me a lot about selling myself.

Bottom line, most schools do the internship thing really well, and you're a knucklehead if you don't check out these resources.

Calling on Parents and Friends

Looking for an internship is *not* like looking for a job. The bar is much lower. It's a temporary role. Usually employers are not paying you, and they get to feel good about making a difference in a young person's life. That's why you should definitely use your parents and their network of friends to explore opportunities.

About one-third of the recent grads I interviewed secured internships through connections provided by their parents. If your family and your friends' parents have professional networks, ask them to go to bat for you. You'll still need to sell yourself. All they're doing is providing the introduction, and maybe a character reference. ("Oh yeah, my son was definitely acquitted on those charges of hacking the registrar's computer system.")

Before deciding whether to take an internship through a family friend, make sure it's going to be a productive learning experience (See "How to Avoid a Wasted Internship" in Chapter 8.). Don't take an offer until you've had a frank discussion about your duties and what you hope to learn. You don't want to waste a summer with someone who is just doing a favor for your parents.

Where to Search for Internships Online

Your career services office will direct you to online resources they like, but here are some popular ones.

www.Internships.com—Most often cited as the leading site for finding internships. Its entire focus is matching students and employers. One important advantage of the site is it lets you search for internships using a variety of criteria to narrow your focus.

www.Idealist.org—An excellent place to find internships in nonprofit organizations. Idealist.org draws from more than 57,000 nonprofit and community organizations in 180 countries.

www.Experience.com—This site includes an extensive section on internships. Its strengths are the free advice and coaching available from people who have been there.

www.Indeed.com—This is a search engine for job listings and internships collected from job boards, newspapers, and company career pages. Look for internships by location and get email alerts when new ones are posted.

www.usajobs.gov/studentjobs—Want an internship in the federal government? This is a good place to get started.

www.goabroad.com/intern-abroad—Visit this site to find an internship that combines work experience and travel outside of the U.S.

Cold Calling Can Create Hot Opportunities

Sometimes the best way to find an internship is just to identify target organizations that you want to work with and reach out to them directly. In the sales world they call this "cold calling." Lily, an art history major at University of California, Santa Barbara, was

300 miles away from where she wanted to intern to learn about the art business. Lily tried cold calling to find a position that would give her experience.

> *I started googling art museums in San Francisco and I systemati-cally wrote to each one asking about summer positions. It turns out to be extremely hard to get internships in the city's museums because kids going to school locally had preferential connections. So then I contacted art galleries, and I ended up getting two internships that summer at very different kinds of places. That was a turning point in my understanding of art as a retail business.*

If you're attending the University of Maryland or the University of Virginia and looking for a summer assignment in Washington, D.C., no problem. Your school's internships office will have many options if you don't wait too long. But, say you're at the University of Florida and want a software marketing internship in Seattle. Forget it. You're on your own. Geographic location can matter a lot when looking for internships.

Once you identify organizations where you might want to intern, do your research. You need to understand their business, products, and services, and then match what you can offer to what they might need. For an exploratory internship, it might be a general pitch like: "As a sociology major at the University, I'm anxious to learn more about marketing careers in consumer products companies like yours. I'm a strong writer, very organized, and a quick learner. Can we meet to explore the possibilities of interning with your company or department?"

In an ideal world, your research will identify a specific area where you think you can help the organization. "My Web research indicates your company is currently making limited use of social media and, perhaps, I could help you accelerate this effort. While majoring in psychology at the University, I was responsible for using social media to promote the school's theater productions…"

Using LinkedIn to Find Internships

A key step in cold calling any company (really "cold emailing") is identifying a specific person to approach. LinkedIn has made this task much easier. Once you have an account on LinkedIn (See Chapter 13.), use the advanced search function to find specific people to approach in your target company.

Here's a useful tip: add your school and target company under keywords in the LinkedIn "Advanced Search" section. This way you'll find employees working there who are alumni of your school. Research these people on the Internet to find their email address. Be sure to mention any mutual connection, e.g., schools or acquaintances in the subject line with details in the first sentence. For example, your subject line could read: "Colorado student exploring internships in sales."

And the first sentence of your email: "As a junior at UC-Boulder, I'm looking for an internship where I can learn about sales operations in beer distributorships. Could we schedule a brief call so I could get your advice about how to explore an internship with your organization?" If you go to school in Boulder and want to work in beer sales, you're golden. At last check, there were 97 people working at Anheuser-Busch with ties to the University of Colorado. You're bound to find someone there who will talk to you about internship possibilities. And won't your parents be proud!

Know How to Close the Deal

Your goal with these emails or phone calls is *always* to get a face-to-face meeting with someone in the company who might help you explore internship possibilities. If distance makes meeting impractical, then try for a Skype call or at least a phone appointment. Your job then is to sell yourself. (See Chapter 16 for more tips on interviewing.)

Be prepared to explain your interests and objectives for an internship and probe for ways you can help the company while you're there. Bigger companies are more likely to have formal internship programs. They are used to bringing people in for different learning experiences. If you're approaching a small organization, they may be less familiar with how an internship could work for them. In this case, you'll need a longer conversation about how an internship could be structured and what you could do for the company while you're there.

Why Internships are Just Like Dating

An internship is like a date. You don't go out with someone unless you think you're going to be entertained, find romance, or at least make your friends jealous because you're hanging with a real hottie. It's the same with internships. Despite what career counselors tell you, organizations won't invite you in unless they think they'll get something in return. Maybe they get to check you out as a potential future employee, or they think you'll do some routine data entry while you're there. Maybe you bring a special skill (e.g., social media or research capabilities) to help them solve a problem. When trying to land an internship, keep asking how can I make it worthwhile for this company to bring me in? Why am I a better choice than the other people competing for this internship?

And, even if you land that internship, what matters is making it pay off in your future job search. How to get the most out of your internships is the focus of Chapter 8.

Checklist for Action:
Score the Right Internship

____1. **Make an appointment at your school's career services or internship programs office.** If you're feeling overwhelmed or confused, schedule a meeting with a counselor to help you think through different options. Talking to someone about how to interpret different internship offerings in a database will save you tons of time and give you a lot more insight about where to apply.

____2. **Ask your parents for names of family friends you could talk to about internship possibilities.** Chances are your parents would love to help you with this. If they have connections, take advantage of them in this job market. This is not cheating!

____3. **Start searching online internship databases.** Your school will recommend some electronic resources. Ask your friends what websites worked for them.

____4. **Ask older students and recent grads about positive internship experiences they've had.** Did they have an internship that sounds like a good fit for you? Ask them to provide you with an introduction.

____5. **Start early if you're going to be cold calling for an internship.** It can often take several months to get the interviews and approvals needed to set up an internship on your own.

CHAPTER EIGHT

Four Ways to Make Your Internships Pay Off

When it comes to job hunting, successful new grads do four things to make internships pay off.

1. Choose Internships Carefully

When you need an internship for course credit or to pacify your parents over the summer, it's tempting to take the first thing that comes along. That may work out for you, but you're much better off answering these important questions first:

- Will this internship give you the knowledge and skills to make you a more attractive job candidate? (You could have this conversation with someone at your potential internship site or someone who knows the types of jobs you might pursue.)

- Will an influential person supervise you during your internship? It's much better to get a recommendation from a director of marketing than an entry-level marketing assistant.

- Will the network of new contacts you gain from this internship help you in your future job search?

When deciding on an internship opportunity, if possible, negotiate a title similar to the type of job you may be looking for in the future. Depending on your career interests, for example, you may want to be called a "marketing intern," "research intern," or "social media intern." Future hiring managers will scan your resume and unless they see a title that matches the job they're trying to fill, they're likely to pass you over.

Finally, you need to have a variety of experiences through your internships. Think twice before you go back to the same place to intern again, unless you will have distinctly different assignments and learn new skills. For example, Katherine, a communications major at the University of Texas, returned to the same animal health products distributor when she could move from the human resources department to an e-commerce role.

How to Avoid a Wasted Internship

So you've found a potential internship, maybe through a family friend or at a Fortune 500 company. Now you absolutely must ask four key questions *before* you accept, says John Wilpers, founder of Degrees2Dreams.com, and an internship expert. Clarifying the answers to these questions increases the chances this experience will make you a stronger candidate in future job searches.

1. *"Can you give me a list of my duties in this internship? What kind of things will I be expected to do?"*

Avoid internships where your sponsor remains vague about what you will be doing. Your goal is to at least do some substantive work so you can demonstrate specific skills to a potential employer. Did you research and write a report, help improve an important office process, or develop content for the company's website?

2. *"Can you tell me about the characteristics of your most successful interns in the past?"* (This assumes they used them previously.)

What will you need to do to be successful as an intern at this company? Listen carefully to the response to your question. There are plenty of big-name companies that will put interns into useless roles. This question lets the hiring manager know you want to do well, and very few interns ask this.

3. *"Who will be my boss and whom will I be spending most of my time with?"*

Ideally, you want your internship sponsor to be a manager whose title makes her or him a great reference, not an entry-level employee who could have been your fraternity brother last year. And you want access to this sponsor at least a couple times a week, so they get to know you and you learn from them.

4. *If the internship is unpaid or low paying, ask yourself: Can I really make it work economically?*

This is obviously a dilemma for recent grads, or even undergrads, who need to support themselves. Are you going into fields like fashion, journalism, marketing, public relations, entertainment or nonprofits? Then you need to expect that unpaid post-college internships are now a standard part of the recent college grad's career path. How will you pay for this?

2. Take Charge of Your Learning

There's a fine line between being eager to learn and being seen as obnoxious or high-maintenance by a busy boss. Pablo recalls how he asserted himself:

After my junior year at Union College, I landed an internship with a small hedge fund in New Jersey. On my first day, the portfolio manager handed me a laptop and suggested I work in an empty room nearby. But the firm's Bloomberg terminal near the research staff was clearly where the action was. So I planted myself there. Before long it became my desk, and the director of research was asking me to use the terminal to research stocks and build financial models. I learned more in that ten weeks than in all of college about how the investment industry works.

An internship provides you with unique access and an opportunity to learn while you are temporarily part of an organization. You need to maximize your learning while you're there. Often, your sponsor will be busy and unsure about how much work you can handle. If you're not getting useful tasks, be politely aggressive and imaginative in suggesting how you might help the organization improve things. You may have to bend some rules to find opportunities to take on more challenging tasks. The easiest way to do this is to come in early or stay late, making it clear you're eager for extra assignments.

Remember, your goals, if possible, are to produce output or results and to develop skills you can point to in future job interviews as things you have shown you can do. For example:

- "I trained eight managers on how to use WordPress blogging software."

- "I researched and wrote a report analyzing our competitor's products in potential new markets."

- "I worked on the team that redesigned the social media strategy for our division."

Managers will almost always respect extra effort and initiative. It helps you stand out from the crowd. They probably still won't offer you a job at the end of your stay, but your eagerness to learn and help the organization will certainly get you a good reference for your resume.

3. Use Internships to Expand Your Network

As soon as you start an internship, begin developing a hit list of people in the company you want to talk to. You can approach virtually anyone there for an informational interview. "Hi, I'm an intern in sales this month, and I'd like to learn how you became marketing director. Could we meet to talk about that and I'd like to get your advice on...(whatever you want to learn about)." Bring questions to each meeting. It shows you're serious and you value their time.

The Drunk Intern

Lucas, a television major at the University of Texas, was in the second week of his internship with an international television production company co-founded by a famous director. Lucas had long viewed this director as a role model for what he hoped would be a career directing live television events like the Super Bowl halftime show. The director was away when Lucas moved to town for the internship and they had not met yet. One night, a fun-loving British producer who Lucas was working for invited him out and kept feeding him drinks. The young intern accepted the refills not wanting to disappoint his boss.

When Lucas went to take a call, he suddenly realized how drunk he was. Returning to the bar, he discovered the producer had been joined by his hero—the rock-star director! Lucas recalled sheepishly, "I'm standing there star-struck. The first thing I say is, 'My dream is to have a career like yours.' Then I couldn't say another word because I was too drunk."

Remember, an internship is an ongoing job interview. You never know when you're going to bump into an opportunity—or your hero. Internships are about building important relationships. To do that you really need to stay sober!

4. Treat Internships Like an Ongoing Job Interview

Your goals as an intern are to build your network and make yourself memorable in a positive way. You never know when the chance to create a good impression will arise.

Andrew majored in English and theater at Bowdoin College and took a series of long-term substitute teaching assignments in New York City schools.

I always behaved in a way that would cultivate job placement. Whenever I walked into the school I would say "Hi" to everyone. I learned the security guards' names. I wanted to make sure everyone there had laughed with me and that they'd experienced me as a good listener. So after a while there was a buzz around this new student teacher.

At the very least, you want to leave your internship with a sparkling recommendation and the possibility of a reference. In some cases, you will want to immediately add this recommendation to your LinkedIn profile (See Chapter 13.).

When Pablo completed his summer internship with a small hedge fund, the CEO gave him a very nice letter of recommendation. Returning to school for senior year, he immediately sent copies of the letter to his growing network with a cover note saying, "Here's what I've done this summer. Will you please keep me in mind if you hear of opportunities of job openings where I could be a potential candidate?"

Every internship is an audition. Like it or not, you are always being evaluated. Are you a hard worker? Do you learn fast? Are you a fun colleague? Would we want you in this organization full time? Whether your boss offers you a job or not, these are questions this person must answer when deciding what kind of recommendation to give you. This is an assignment you definitely want to ace.

Checklist for Action:
Maximize the Value of Your Internships

____ 1. **Compare several internship opportunities to decide which one you will benefit from the most.** Where will you gain the most skills and best references? Don't take the first and easiest thing that comes along. (See stories in "Special Section: Search Strategies That Paid Off" for ideas on using internships strategically.)

____ 2. **Be politely pushy when looking for additional opportunities to learn during your internship.** Your boss is extremely busy and unsure how much you can handle. Help her or him with the routine stuff and then ask for more challenging tasks.

____ 3. **Set a goal of one or two detailed conversations— informational interviews—per week with people in the organization who can offer insights from their own careers and advice on how to start your own.**

____ 4. *Never* **forget to ask for a recommendation from your boss when your internship ends.** If they are willing, but extremely busy, offer to draft a recommendation for them to edit. This is common practice today. It is *not* cheating!

CHAPTER NINE

Beyond Internships: Great Alternatives for Building Your Resume

Internships get most of the attention, but they're not the only way to make your resume stand out. You may consider other opportunities such as volunteering, doing research with professors, and working for pay.

Volunteer: Give Yourself to Get Experience

Whether you're considered an intern or a volunteer is usually more a matter of how an organization thinks of you. Volunteering, a common practice in the nonprofit sector, is a valuable way to build a resume.

While Sara, a Beloit College grad, was looking for a fundraising position with nonprofits in Chicago, she volunteered once a week to learn how to use specific database software, making her more valuable to potential employers. Carlos' volunteer efforts in an inner-city tutoring program, while a senior at the University of Maryland, gave him experience and confidence that helped him work with middle schoolers after graduating.

Finding volunteer positions is easier than landing an internship because most nonprofits and many public-sector organizations are set up to welcome volunteers on a regular basis. Here's a tip: try using your volunteer position to request informational interviews with senior leaders in the organization. Even better, find out who is on the board of directors and ask for a meeting. Since you're already giving something to their organization, board members are much more than likely to be willing to offer career advice and contacts.

Build Knowledge: Conduct Research with Professors

Obviously, if you're thinking about graduate school in the future, doing research with one of your professors is a good way to get experience and a reference to make your application stronger. A research project also can deepen your knowledge about topics important to employers, if it's relevant to the industry or field you want to pursue. Pablo, a Union College economics and philosophy major, intentionally undertook an investment-based senior thesis to help his job search. He explains:

> I wanted to write a thesis that I could show to people interviewing me. That way I could say, "Not only did I work for a company last summer that does this kind of investing, but here is an analysis I did on banks in the Northeast."

One word of caution: if you want a research project to strengthen your resume, make sure the topic is likely to be relevant to potential employers. That means it can't be too academic, too abstract or too big.

> Carl was an economics major at Colorado College when he committed to a research project analyzing stock data for portfolios with more than three million data points. This proved way

too ambitious for an undergrad thesis. So, instead of having impressive research to show potential employers, Carl spent months after graduation trying to salvage his ill-conceived thesis.

If you want a research project to be a useful addition to your resume, get advice on the practicality and value of your topic. Test the idea on other professors, your parents and, ideally, some people in the industry where you want to work.

Make Your Part-Time Job Pay Off Later

If an internship won't cut it and you just need to earn money, there are still options to consider that can improve your resume in the process. Not all jobs are created equal in terms of building a resume.

- *Lily worked for three years at Jamba Juice on the UCLA campus making smoothies. It was a fun job, but didn't help much in looking for work after college.*

- *Yong had a job for four years at the University of Florida providing on-campus IT support. Most potential employers really valued this.*

- *Faith found her job creating marketing materials for the university's recreation department gave her important additional pieces for her graphic design portfolio.*

There are specific things you can do to increase the payoff of the work experience you get while in school:

Plan ahead when picking an on-campus job. If you have a choice, choose one that allows you to create results you can show to potential employers, or one that builds your network. Some campus jobs that can enhance your job search include university tour guide, which develops speaking and presentation skills, or working in career services or alumni affairs to increase networking opportunities and access to internships. By the way, students who work in the career services office invariably get good job offers.

Look for local jobs in a field related to your post-college career. After acing his news-writing course, Tyler scored a job as a part-time reporter with a local newspaper because his journalism professor worked there. You might find administrative work with a local investment advisor, insurance broker or other small company. This might be called an internship even though your primary goal is to make money. Just don't ever overlook the chances this work presents for building your marketable skills.

Can you work virtually for an employer? Lots of small companies today are hiring young people to set up websites and run social media campaigns. This work can often be done from your dorm room. Writing part-time for specialized websites also is a potential income source if you have adequate subject expertise and the contacts with site owners or editors.

Tip: *Check out the HubSpot certification program at http:// inboundmarketing.com/university/certification. This free online program teaches you best practices in blogging, social media, search engine optimization, etc., which will give you confidence to provide these basic services to small businesses.*

Start a new business either on campus or at home during the summer. Tobias, a finance and computer science major at Brandeis University, started a website design business one summer when he couldn't find the finance internship he wanted. Zach, a Colby College history major, started and ran a car-detailing business in his hometown during his summer breaks. He also helped purchase and revive an on-campus laundry business. He says:

"It's easy for my generation to blame their lack of experience on the economic climate. But I was able to say, 'The economy stinks. Still, I've started two successful businesses.' You learn everything starting a business. That's how I figured out what I wanted to do. I learned the aspects of business I really like are sales, business development, and marketing. And, in interviews I could show how my sales skills made these businesses successful."

Pay Attention to Your Experiences

Going to college is about getting more experience in academic, social, and worldly pursuits. Until recently, these lessons weren't expected to prepare you for specific jobs immediately upon graduation, especially from a liberal arts program. But that expectation has changed. The objective—and opportunity—of a college education now must include more attention to having experiences that develop the knowledge and skills valued by employers.

As a student, your job in college is to make sure you get as many valuable experiences as you can through courses, internships, and other methods described here. Experience, however, is simply not enough to get you a great job. You may know what kind of work you want, and have experience that qualifies you as a good candidate. But you also need a network of contacts to help you find opportunities and stand out in the eyes of managers with jobs to fill. Otherwise, your potential will go unnoticed. How do you get the connections you need to get hired? The next three chapters show how to build and use networks to land a job much faster.

Checklist for Action:
Identify Resume-building Opportunities

____1. Look for opportunities to volunteer in organizations
where you will get ideas and connections related to future
work interests. Identify fields you want to learn about, skills you
want to acquire, or people you want to meet. Many organizations will call you an intern, but in others you'll be a volunteer.
Don't be confused by the labels. Focus on what you can learn
and who can become an ally in your future job-search network.

____2. Talk to your professors about collaborating on research,
if deeper knowledge in your field will differentiate you from
other students. Just make sure the topic will be of interest to
future employers. Professors usually pursue research that interests them, not the outside world. Make sure any project you
work on is relevant to your future interests.

____3. Choose part-time jobs with an eye to the skills you can
develop and show on your resume. As a rule, any job is better
than none. But becoming a stronger public speaker as a campus
tour guide is better than being an expert barista. All part-time
jobs are not created equal in terms of their value in your
post-college job search.

____4. Consider alternative forms of employment, such as
starting your own business or working virtually for a company that already knows you.

____5. Avoid easy money schemes like the plague! Online
gambling, network marketing, and Internet marketing scams
are popular traps. They almost always cost you or others serious
money and add nothing to your resume.

Make Connections

Why people, not resumes, are your most valuable job-hunting resources...and how to build your go-to networking list.

CHAPTER TEN

Networking: How it Really Helps You Land a Job

"I thought networking was just finding an alum's email and begging them for an informational interview. But I've learned networking is so much more, and that was never explained to me."
—*Andrew, Bowdoin College,*
New York City high-school teacher

"To get the job you want you have to push out of your comfort zone and go for it."
— *Zoey, Central Michigan University,*
event-planning coordinator

"When I was starting my job search in college I thought I don't need networking. As a result, I didn't do a good job finding positions to apply for. I wish I'd known better."
—*Tobias, Brandeis University, Google contractor*

If you take only one thing away from this book, it should be this: building, using, and maintaining an effective network is the most important thing you can do to ensure a successful job search in today's market.

B y "networking" I don't mean communicating more on Facebook, Pinterest, or Twitter. It goes much deeper than that. Networking means developing relationships with people who like you enough to try to help you directly or indirectly in finding a job. Networking is not about using people, being a loser because you can't do it on your own, and it's not cheating on your classmates because knowing someone gives you an advantage in looking for work. Every person who is famous or successful in his or her professional life has gotten where they are by developing and using a network of friends, supporters, and colleagues.

The next three chapters are a short course on networking. They will not only show you why networking is so critical to your job, but they'll also help you understand whom you want to connect with and how to do it as productively as possible.

Networking 101

If you're feeling lost, overwhelmed, or intimidated when it comes to networking for a job search, you can get extra help from these resources:

1. *Highly Effective Networking: Meet the Right People and Get a Great Job* by Orville Pierson, Career Press, 2009. This practical book by a real pro shows how to develop a relatively low-key systematic approach to leveraging the network you already have.

2. *I Got My Dream Job and So Can You* by Pete Leibman, Amacom, 2012. This book focuses a lot on the importance of building relationships to get a job and is full of dynamite networking tips.

3. *The Skinny on Networking: Maximize the Power of Numbers* by Jim Randel, Rand Media, 2010. If you're not a reader, but need to improve your networking skills, this is the book for you. It's billed as a quick, fun read.

4. *The Networking Survival Guide: Practical Advice to Help You Gain Confidence, Approach People, and Get the Success You Want* by Diane Darling, McGraw-Hill, 2010. Provides nitty-gritty tips for meeting and talking to people from an expert who regularly speaks to college audiences.

5. Ask about "how-to-network" resources at your career services office. Schools realize the importance of this skill and are likely to have materials and counselors who can help you.

How Networking Gets You a Job

Networking can solve four specific problems when you're trying to find a job:

1. Figure out what kind of job you want.
2. Find promising positions to apply for.
3. Get your resume noticed.
4. Obtain the inside track on specific jobs.

Network to clarify what job you want

You can't conduct a successful job search when you're unsure what types of jobs you want to pursue. Networking helps with that. Here's how it worked for Anna, a political science major at UCLA.

I was interested in public health, and it turned out my neighbor had a friend who worked in a nonprofit research center focused on women's health. So I contacted her and she invited me to talk with different women in the center about their careers. Most of

95

the women had their masters in public health, but they had gone different routes. All of them said I should work before getting a masters. It was also great to talk to some of the younger women who hadn't gone back for a masters. They said sometimes it's good to just get an administrative job because if a more interesting position opens up they'll offer it to you.

Talking with people who have experience in fields you might be interested in is a great way to get insights about what kind of job you want and what career path you might take.

Network to identify specific job opportunities

Even if you know the industries and types of jobs you want to focus on, you need to find specific positions to apply for where you will be a viable candidate. Without this information you can't connect your skills and interests to what employers need. Talking to people who may know about particular organizations and job openings that are right for you is often the solution. The U.S. Bureau of Labor Statistics estimates 70% of jobs are found through this type of networking.

Faith networked continually after graduating from James Madison University as she tried to land a job in graphic design. Her father met the head of a small design firm at a community service event in Baltimore and encouraged her to contact him.

I emailed Greg and said I'd love to have an informational inter-view because I knew they already had a designer. We went to lunch and he asked me about the internships I'd had and what I'd done. He said he was very impressed with my portfolio. He said he'd be in touch. Two weeks later I got an email from Greg saying their designer was moving to New York, and I was the first person he thought of for the job. I tell people you never know what connection is going to get you a job.

Network to draw special attention to your resume

How do you separate yourself from the crowd? Daniel was about to graduate from Penn State as a political science major when a key connection helped his resume get noticed.

I got connected with a Penn State alum working at the Department of Justice. He offered to pass my resume along to the paralegal supervisor. That definitely helped me get the job. I found out later that the paralegal program relies heavily on current employees passing on resumes.

Connecting with people who can personally approach a hiring manager on your behalf is an essential benefit of networking today. This doesn't mean you'll get the job, but it greatly increases your chances of being seriously considered.

Network to get the inside track on a job

Getting your resume special attention is one thing, but sometimes knowing the right people creates a much clearer path to a new job. Tobias, an economics and computer science major at Brandeis University, scored a temporary job as a contractor at Google this way.

I found out this guy who had gone to my high school was working at Google. So I called him and said, "I'd like to talk with you about what you do and figure out if there might be a place for me in Google." I met with him and he had me meet with some others in the company. About a month later, he said they had an open position. I started working there a week later.

The most productive benefit of networking is when a relationship connects you directly to a job and minimizes concerns about your character and qualifications. This often leads to a much faster hiring decision.

Networking can solve four of your biggest job-search problems, but where should you start your networking efforts? Well, that's the focus of Chapter 11.

CHAPTER ELEVEN

Where to Make Career-building Connections

"More business decisions occur over lunch and dinner than at any other time, yet no...courses are given on the subject."
—Peter Drucker, management expert

This chapter provides the basics on where to find the contacts you need to get employed.

Where Should I Network?

You have access to a much bigger network of people who can help you than you realize. Guaranteed. Who you reach out to depends on your objectives at this stage of your job search. Are you still uncertain about what you want to do? Or do you know the specific organizations and jobs you want to go after? Your situation will dictate what kinds of connections you need to make. And if you're thinking networking is all too awkward or intimidating, don't worry. See "Networking for Introverts" in Chapter 12.

Modern family networking

Like it or not, your parents and relatives are probably your best sources of networking contacts. About 50% of those I interviewed had major networking help from their parents or close relatives. However, you must give your family permission to help you. Offer them some guidance on the types of contacts you're looking for. Try brainstorming about people they know that could provide useful advice or contacts. They may come up with names that positively make you cringe. Uncle Louie retired from the Post Office 10 years ago and lives for new episodes of "Dancing with the Stars." He is a bad bet. But that annoying neighbor with the awful outfits might be a successful salesman with some very useful ideas and contacts.

To get your parent's help with networking, give them a short script on how to talk about you. That's because they may not understand the field you're exploring. For example:

"My son is a student at the U. and wants to learn more about career opportunities in sports management (or whatever). Will you talk to him to share your experiences and ideas? And how should he contact you?"

"Our daughter just graduated from…She's looking for a job in healthcare marketing. Could you talk to her about what you do and maybe brainstorm about organizations or people she should approach?"

You will no doubt wince at some of your family's seemingly awkward suggestions, but follow through anyway. Andrew was struggling to find work in New York City after being forced to leave a disastrous first job in a nonprofit:

My Mom went to a birthday party with a family friend in Boston and discovered their nephew's wife was in charge of hiring substitute teachers in New York City. When Mom suggested I contact this person, I thought, "Oh, God." But I rolled my eyes and then called anyway. The woman was really excited. She wanted me to send my resume right away. That's how my teaching career started.

What are friends for?

By now, you likely have friends and acquaintances from college, your hometown, summer camp, and other places you've spent time. All of these people have parents and other connections they can link you to. Whether you're looking for ideas about career direction or for contacts in specific industries, don't overlook the introductions friends can provide. Rachel, an English and economics major at Trinity College, got some great advice from her roommate's mother:

She's a lawyer and on a long car ride back to school during junior year she helped me understand what credentials I'd need if I wanted to combine business and law. She gave me specifics, like if I wanted to apply to law school I needed to do this. And to work in investment banking, I needed to start emailing people now. These were things I never would have known.

Again, you'll have to give your friends some ideas about what kind of help you're looking for to make progress on your job search.

"Could I talk to your Mom about her career in advertising?"

"Can I ask your Dad if he knows anybody who works in environmental nonprofits?"

These are easy conversations to have because your friends' parents will be anxious to help you if they can. They're likely to provide direct introductions to people who can be even more helpful. Pablo used this approach very effectively with friends when looking for a job in finance. He was surprised his classmates didn't do the same.

I never understood why my friends weren't meeting with more people who had experience. My Dad has been doing his job for 30 years and he's glad to share what he's learned. But I think only one person took me up on it.

Contacts from previous internships & jobs

Any place you have interned or worked in the last few years is an important source of networking contacts. If you've had a successful internship, even though the organization can't hire you, often your old boss will brainstorm about possible connections to help in your job search. If you know you're going to be starting a job search within the next year, a great question to ask colleagues when wrapping up an internship is: "Can you give me any names of people I could contact for advice as I start my search for...?" If they say "yes," then ask if they'd be willing to provide an email introduction.

Alumni from your school

This is probably the most overlooked source of networking connections available to college students and recent grads. Everyone who went to your school is fair game as a networking resource. And the odds are they will be glad to help you if they can. LinkedIn (See Chapter 13 for details.) makes it incredibly easy to find alumni from your school who are working in the businesses you are interested in.

If you are attending Ohio State, for example, and want to explore opportunities in financial services around Cleveland, LinkedIn lists more than 300 people with ties to your school who you could contact. Here's one that should be harder. Say you've graduated from the University of Florida and want to find a job in public relations in Chicago. LinkedIn still shows dozens of people with ties to UF in the Chicago area you could approach after doing additional research on them.

Other networking resources

There are many other places to look for contacts that can help you, but those above are most frequently mentioned. They also are the easiest place to start and most likely to respond favorably to requests for help. Others to consider include:

102

Faculty—Your English professor, for example, might have helpful insights and contacts for jobs that involve writing. Be sure to ask faculty members about former students of theirs who have done well since leaving school.

Religious leaders—Ask your pastor or rabbi, for example, if he or she knows people in the congregation you could be introduced to.

Sports & hobbies—One effective way to grow your network is to join clubs or groups that attract people who can help in your job search. Carl, for example, made great contacts with managers in the finance industry when he joined a squash club in Minneapolis. Soon he had his new squash partners passing around his resume.

Business executives/professionals you don't know—Cold calls are the hardest way to build your network, but they also can be highly productive. If you identify someone who might help in your job search, research them on Google and LinkedIn and send them a customized email.

Career fairs & formal networking events—These events are quite intimidating, but they also can pay off big time. Taylor, a psychology major at the University of Illinois, discovered the value of networking events late in her college career:

Walking into my first career fair senior year I wished so badly that it wasn't my first one. I wished I had known so I could have gone to these events, even as a sophomore, to start making myself familiar to the companies there. Even if it didn't seem important then, I could have learned from it. My roommate also told me about the American Marketing Association and we joined together. That was great exposure because once a month a company would come speak to the group and I put it on my resume.

You can connect with the right people to jump start your job search, once you know where to find them. But how do you get these people to help you? That's the focus of Chapter 12.

Checklist for Action:
Uncover Networking Opportunities

____1. **Write down your purpose for networking now.** Are you trying to meet with people to help you decide what kind of job to pursue? Are you looking for assistance identifying specific opportunities? Or are you looking for someone who can give you the inside track on a specific job?

____2. **Ask your parents (or other family members) if they know people you can talk to.** Give them a brief script to help them explain to their friends what exactly you're looking for.

____3. **Talk to your friends about what their parents do.** Even if it doesn't sound too promising, set up a call or meeting with them anyway. Use it as a practice interview. Your friends' parents will be anxious to help you if they can. They'd want someone to do it for their kid after all.

____4. **Make a list of people from previous internships and jobs who could be helpful. See Chapter 12 for tips on how to approach them.**

____5. **Schedule meetings with a couple of faculty members and ask them for career advice and others they could introduce you to.**

____6. **Check with your school's career services office about resources they have for connecting with alumni.** Many universities now sponsor networking events to help you meet people. Or use LinkedIn to find alumni in fields or companies of interest.

___**7. Don't be a knucklehead.** Check out at least one career fair and other networking event sponsored by your school. You'll learn stuff, even if the event is lame. Ask questions. Act interested. If nothing else, you'll learn what fields and companies you *don't* want to work in.

CHAPTER TWELVE

Beyond Facebook: How to Build Relationships That Get You Employed

Your ability to make solid connections with strangers who can help you is critical in a successful job search. Persuading people to assist you, however, is not a skill that comes naturally.

Every once in a while you meet someone at a party, or sit next to someone on a plane and voila—it turns out this person has ideas and connections that can be a huge help. You definitely want to take advantage of those situations. But most of the time, these career-related conversations, often called "informational interviews," must be actively pursued.

Ironically, your goal in these meetings is *never* to ask for a job. It is, rather, to learn more about particular industries, types of work, and to uncover potential opportunities to explore. How do you build new relationships that will add momentum to your job search? Read on.

Four Ways to Grow & Maintain Your Search Network

1. Convince people to want to help you

Networking is a lot like setting a friend up on a blind date. You wouldn't want to introduce your friend to a loser. Well, now you're the potential blind date. And you've got to convince your new networking contact you are worth introducing to others.

In Pete Leibman's terrific book, *I Got My Dream Job and So Can You*, he nails it when he describes the things to do to get people to like you. According to Leibman, you must be:

Real—It's more important to be yourself than to try to be cool and overly solicitous. Appearing a little nervous is real and even somewhat charming. Acting like you know it all is annoying.

Enthusiastic—If you are genuinely enthusiastic about meeting with someone and learning from that person, you're taking a huge step in building that relationship. Your eagerness must be genuine or people will be turned off.

Curious—Asking interesting, insightful questions is a great way to engage people. Demonstrate that you've done your homework and you're anxious to learn from their experiences and advice.

Appreciative—Let people know how much you appreciate their time. Always take some notes, even if what they're saying doesn't seem important to you. It's an insult to ask people for their time and not to jot down some of what they're saying. Be sure to send a thank you—a handwritten note is best, an email will do.

Professional—Be on time, clean, and dress nicely. Not the way your grandmother prefers, but remember you need to impress this person enough so he or she will feel comfortable recommending you to others. And lose the word "like." "Like, your network won't, like, grow if you sound this way when you, like, talk to people."

Offer something in return—Relationships are built on mutual benefit. You will stand out if you look for ways to give back to those people you meet in your job-search networking. Toward the end of your conversation ask, "Is there any way I can help you? I'm talking to a lot of people these days. Are there questions you have that I could ask others?" In addition, is there a book or article you think might be of interest to the person you're meeting? A research paper you've written at school that you'd be glad to share? Look for little ways to try to return the favor of meeting with you. They will probably say, "no." But they will greatly appreciate your offer.

How to Land Informational Interviews

To get an informational interview, send an introductory email or hand-written note saying how you're connected to the person (if it's not obvious) and ask to meet them for 20 minutes. The note might say:

- *"Dear _____, I am contacting you at _____'s suggestion."*

  —Use Mr. or Ms. unless you know them very well. Older people get really annoyed at Gen-Ys acting overly casual. Better to err on the formal side.
  —Be sure your first sentence indicates *who* suggested you contact them.
  —Never abbreviate or use texting short hand. And never, ever start with "Hey." You are asking to have an adult conversation about work and careers. Lose the sloppy grammar and spelling you share with friends. Practice sounding professional.

- *"I am currently exploring career and work opportunities in _____."*

  —Specify the field (financial services, nonprofits, wineries) or function (marketing, sales, public relations, investment management).

- *"Could we meet for 20 minutes in the next few weeks so I could learn from your career experiences...?"* (*Add a phrase relevant to them: ...in marketing, or ...at Taco Bell.*)

—Only ask for a little of their time to minimize any resistance to scheduling a meeting. Unless they are unusually busy or you come off as a distracted goof ball, they will likely give you more time than you ask for.

- *"I would welcome your advice and direction as I explore work opportunities to pursue after I graduate from _____."*

—This is the key phrase because people love giving advice based on their experience. Believe it or not, you're surrounded by people who want to help you if they can. You just have to ask for what they can give you, which is advice that will be helpful as you figure out what kind of job you want and where to pursue it.

- *"Please suggest a day and time that is convenient for a meeting or a phone call."*

—Always go for a face-to-face meeting. It's a much better way to build rapport, and you'll often get more time that way. Phone calls or Skype are acceptable alternatives when distance is a factor.

—Be sure to write "Referred by _____" in the email subject line. *There are a million reasons people will miss the first message and none have to do with not wanting to talk to you.* If the person doesn't respond within a week, send the message again, adding "2nd try:" in front of the original subject line. Try a third time if you don't hear after another week.

2. Get good at making new connections

Almost everyone you're trying to meet these days is extremely busy, so be savvy about the approach you use to schedule a meeting. Carl, a Colorado College grad, spent a year building a new network in Minneapolis to land a job in finance. After volunteering to work as a financial analyst on a major political campaign, Carl's well-connected boss rewarded his efforts by sending out 20 emails to friends in the investment management industry in Minneapolis. Carl recalls:

Suddenly, I had 15 people willing to meet with me for informational interviews. They didn't know of positions open, but I'd ask them to give me three or four names where they could act as a referral or give me a letter of introduction.

So I'd email these people saying, "So-and-so has encouraged me to reach out to you for advice. If it's convenient I'd love to explore some of your ideas regarding my job search." I had different form letters depending on their industry—hedge fund, investment bank, consulting—with different bullet points about my background. I could customize each message quickly. My network grew exponentially.

In mastering this process of connecting, Carl customized each introductory email so it was clear he understood who his contact worked for. He also had to present his job-search objectives and skills in a way that made sense to investment bankers, consultants, or whomever he was approaching. It only takes a few minutes of research on Google or LinkedIn to personalize the email you're about to send, but the chances of getting a positive response are greatly increased.

Pick up the phone. Another trick Carl learned was to use the phone when he didn't hear back from a potential new networking contact. He recognized that executives get lost in volumes of emails.

111

A phone call often got him a lot further. You may find it helps to have a simple script to follow when you make these calls, so you don't get tongue-tied or embarrassed. For example:

> "Hi, this is Haley Dunphy. I'm contacting you at my Uncle Mitchell's suggestion. I'm exploring my career options since getting kicked out of college. Uncle Mitchell thought you would be a great person to talk to about jobs in retailing. Could we schedule a brief meeting in the next few weeks? My number is..."

You get the picture. Keep it brief, confident, and be clear about what step the other person should take.

Face time is prime time. Recent grads I interviewed consistently advised going for face-to-face meetings because you're likely to get more time once a busy manager sits down with you. Unless you're an inarticulate slob you can sell yourself much better when you're across the desk from someone, instead of catching them in traffic on their cell phone.

Don't take it personally. Never take a "no response" personally. People worth talking to are so busy that it's easy for them to forget or miss an email or a voice mail. If somebody has referred you, politely reach out to your new contact at least three or four times before giving up. People will respect your persistence, as long as you're polite and professional. For example, a week after your first email gets no response, send another. In the subject line write: "2nd try: Referred by..." Then add a sentence at the beginning of your previous message: "I contacted you last week, but didn't hear back so I thought I'd try again."

Networking is *both* a numbers and a quality game. You need to connect with people who can actually hire you. But to get there and to learn enough about your chosen field you need to talk to a lot of people.

After accepting an award at a meeting planner's convention, Zoey's notoriety appeared to be a networking bonanza. At least 100 people gave her their business cards, and 30 said they possibly had a job opening. But when she diligently followed up after the convention, only two openings turned out to be promising opportunities Zoey wanted to pursue. Never pin your hopes on one opportunity or networking contact. Always keep multiple connections and opportunities in play. Too many things can—and often do—go wrong to count on one or two possible jobs. See Chapter 20 to learn how Zoey's story ends.

Create a follow-up system. As your network grows into dozens of contacts, it can start to feel overwhelming. Zach, the Colby College history major looking for a job in commercial real estate, benefitted from an organized approach.

At first I'd just meet with people and that would be the end of it. Being organized makes the whole process much easier. I made a spreadsheet, which showed who I emailed, when we talked on the phone, when we met, and who introduced us. I'd also put in notes on how the meeting went. This way, I could follow up with emails showing contacts I'd actually talked to and others they'd referred me to.

Whether you use index cards, a spreadsheet, or a cool online tool like JibberJobber, find some way to organize and track your growing job-search network. Three months from now, when you are meeting multiple people from the same company or in the same industry, you will need help recalling who you talked to, what you learned, and who they referred you to. Having a system to recall what you've learned will make you sound much smarter than you feel.

Zach's system of tracking his networking contacts also allowed him to call on his growing set of relationships for help. When trying to schedule a meeting with a hard-to-reach executive, he'd view his list of contacts to see who might know this person. Then he'd ask them to shoot the executive an email or make a call to promote the meeting with Zach.

Networking for Introverts

Are you someone who doesn't particularly like meeting new people? Do you hate big social events? Would you rather communicate by email? Then you're probably an introvert, an orientation encouraged today by texting and email technologies. Why have an awkward face-to-face interaction when you can text, right? That approach may work in your social life, but it's career suicide.

The more you avoid face-to-face interactions in your job search, the longer you will be living with your parents. Guaranteed. People help and hire others whom they know and like. The only way someone can really get to know you is by meeting you face-to-face, or at least talking at length by phone.

Here are five things you can do to overcome your natural inclination to avoid networking events and meeting people face-to-face.

1. *Acknowledge your introvert tendencies and commit to counteracting them for the sake of your job search.* Being aware that you'd rather avoid meeting new people is a critical step. Notice when you make excuses for not attending a networking event, or when you put off emailing a promising contact to set up a meeting. You can't change behavior you're not aware of. Remember, no meeting, no job.

2. *Set modest goals at networking events.* Focus on leaving with two promising new connections. Don't worry about "working the room" or collecting dozens of business cards.

3. *Develop and practice a list of questions ahead of time.* For example, an easy one is "How did you get into your current job (or industry)?" If you're meeting someone one-on-one, prepare some written questions ahead of time anyway. If you're going to an event, just have two or three in mind.

4. *Focus on other people by being a good listener.* A lot of discomfort around networking comes from our obsession over how we're seen by others. Did I say something stupid? Do I look nervous? Most people have the same worries. You will help yourself by helping others feel more comfortable. Be curious. Ask people about themselves. Look for common connections around school, sports teams, hometowns, mutual friends, hobbies, etc.

5. *Reach out ahead of time to someone you know who will be at the event.* Before going to a career fair at the University of Texas, Katherine emailed a recruiter she had met the year before at a similar event. She reminded the recruiter of their mutual interest in horses. This connection gave Katherine a place to start her networking conversations. Try to identify a couple of people ahead of time who you can seek out to give yourself a sense of purpose.

If you find yourself continually avoiding face-to-face contacts with new people, there are some excellent resources to help reduce the negative effects on your job search. For example, see:

- *The Introvert's Guide to Success in Business and Leadership* by Lisa Petrilli, C-Level Strategies, 2011.

- Get a free PDF on "Effective Networking for Introverts" at www.RuthSchimel.com

- Google "Networking" and "Introverts" and you'll find you have a lot of company.

3. Always ask for additional introductions

Anytime you go into a meeting—with your uncle, a school alum, or a contact from a previous internship—try to come away with at least three new names. At the end of your meeting, ask who else you might speak to for more help. Then request, "Could you introduce us by email?" If the person hesitates, ask if you can at least use his or her name when you contact this individual.

When brainstorming about possible contacts, politely push for introductions to more senior-level people. It's better to get referred to a vice president or director of marketing, for example, than a marketing assistant. The former are much more likely to know others with the authority to hire you. And then follow up right away on these introductions with an email or call to explain what you are looking for and to ask for a meeting.

4. Keep your network alive

One reason it's important to document your growing list of contacts is, like it or not, you will probably be in the job market again within the next three years. At least some of these people will be worth talking to again. To keep your network actively interested in your success:

Keep people informed of your job search progress. Let them know whom you have met with and what opportunities you're focusing on. Invite them to pass on any information about additional contacts that might be helpful. And, of course, thank them again for their help.

When you land a good job, thank everyone who helped you. People will be pleased to hear this news and reminded that they helped you along the way. You also can provide updated contact information so they know how to keep in touch. Carl spent a year building a new network in Minneapolis. He says:

After I got my job, I shot everyone an email within a week. Everyone who I had met with and who had passed me on to other people, I let them know I had just started working. I thanked them for meeting with me. The networking never stops. Once you build a network it's important not to let it atrophy. Now I might email them every few months just to keep in touch.

Look for reasons to give back to your most helpful contacts. The key to networking is finding ways to help those who help you. Always keep an eye out for articles, links, or contacts that might be of interest to others. That's what networking is all about: continually looking for ways to help others, so they will want to return the favor in the future.

Changes in technology have made networking both easier and more challenging. The next two chapters show you how to take advantage of new tools and how to avoid the technology traps that are undermining the job searches of many new grads.

Checklist for Action:
Expand Your Network

____1. Set a measurable to goal to send out one, three, or even five emails a week requesting informational interviews. Use the script in "How to Land Informational Interviews" as a guide.

____2. If you can schedule meetings with close family friends or parents of your classmates, ask them for honest feedback at the end of your meeting. "What could I do differently to come across more effectively?" In these early safe "practice" conversations look for advice such as: "Try to do more research so you can ask better questions. Don't play with your hair so much. Try to make more eye contact." This can be hard to hear, but it is a gift to you from those who want you to succeed.

____3. When you start having informational interviews, make a firm habit of always asking for three new names of people to contact.

____4. Create a folder on your computer where you save drafts of the different emails you create to introduce yourself to new contacts. You will have to present your job-search objectives and skills to people in different ways and having messages you revise and reuse will save you lots of time.

____5. Make a game out of trying to get a meeting with someone you were referred to but who doesn't respond to your request. Commit to contacting them *at least five times* before giving up. And make two of those contacts by phone. Always be polite and professional. Notice what you learn from this experience.

___6. Create a system to track your contacts so you can follow up. Check out JibberJobber.com to learn about one tool for managing your growing network.

Leverage
Technology

What you *don't* know about applicant tracking and
social media will keep you unemployed longer.

CHAPTER THIRTEEN

Make Applicant Tracking & LinkedIn Work For–Not Against–You

You know a lot about technology, right? You've been using cell phones, communicating on Facebook, and downloading music since middle school. How hard can it be to use technology in a job search? The answer, as they say in Boston, is "wicked hard." In fact, most college students and recent grads have serious misconceptions about how to use computers, smart phones, and the Internet successfully when it comes to getting a job.

Knowing how to use specific applications is essential when you need to:

- Look like a strong job candidate
- Find the best people to network with
- Be more visible to potential employers
- Get a good job as fast as possible

Chapters 13 and 14 show how to use technology to your advantage to get a job faster. Even more important, they teach what you need to know so you won't be handicapped in your search. First, let's see how smart you are. Take the Technology IQ Quiz in the box to learn which sections of these two chapters will be most helpful.

Quiz: What's Your Job-Search Technology IQ?

1. I can explain how an Applicant Tracking System (ATS) works. YES__ NO__

2. My resumes are written to successfully navigate an ATS. YES__ NO__

3. I have a LinkedIn profile. YES__ NO__

4. My LinkedIn profile is 90% complete with recommendations, key words in the right places, and a list of groups I've joined. YES__ NO__

5. I use a Twitter account. YES__ NO__

6. I know how to use Twitter to find networking contacts and job opportunities. YES__ NO__

7. I understand the pros and cons of blogging as part of my search strategy. YES__ NO__

8. I know the pros and cons of online job boards and how *not* to use them. YES__ NO__

9. I understand how my digital footprint could keep me from getting a job and I cleaned up my act. YES__ NO__

10. I know how Facebook can both help and hurt me in my job search. YES__ NO__

Answers to Technology IQ Quiz are at end of chapter

If you have taken the quiz, you know how much—or how little—you know about using technology in your job search. Don't feel bad if you flunked. Most students do. Just because you've been using computers forever doesn't mean you know how to use them when looking for a job. And remember there is a difference between technologies to *get* a job and technologies to *do* a job.

Of course, the computer applications you need to understand will depend on the jobs you're applying for. Unless you are only approaching very small companies, you must know about Applicant Tracking Systems (ATS). Ignorance in this area is the biggest technology pitfall facing job seekers today. And many career counselors don't understand this technology themselves!

If you're applying for a job in a business or nonprofit, you also must have a well-developed LinkedIn profile. Employers won't take you seriously if you don't. But some fields like entertainment and education don't care much about LinkedIn yet. And if you're looking at marketing or public relations jobs, they probably won't even consider you if you don't have a Twitter account. The bottom line is you must research what technologies matter in the fields you're exploring because what employers expect you to know and use changes constantly and differs from job to job.

ATS—Welcome to the Black Hole

Applicant Tracking Systems allow employers to collect, search, screen, and store resumes from job candidates. The good news is, like the Common App you used for college, an ATS makes it easier to apply for lots of jobs fast. The bad news is the chances your resume will actually be seriously considered or that you will get an interview are very low.

An ATS uses automated-screening tools that scan and score your resume, looking for the right job-related key words in the right places. If you have done your homework and used the relevant key words in the right format, then your chances of being considered increase. If you've submitted your standard resume, you're unlikely to hear anything about it. *An ATS is not a social media application. But it is probably the technology that will have the greatest impact on your job search, and most people don't understand it.*

Organizations use an ATS for a variety of reasons. They allow over-worked recruiters to screen and manage hundreds or even thousands of resumes quickly to find promising candidates. They save companies time and money, which is what the boss cares about. In the meantime, dealing with an ATS is a huge headache for job seekers. How hard is it to get through this gauntlet of automation? Talent guru Peter Cappelli reports on one company that had 25,000 applications for a standard engineering position. When the ATS finished screening all the resumes, not one was considered qualified! How is that even possible?

Nine tips to getting your resume read

Here are nine things you can do to increase your chances of getting an interview when your resume is screened by an ATS.

1. Don't apply for jobs that you are clearly unqualified for. One of the reasons companies resort to ATS technology is so many unqualified applicants apply for positions that it overwhelms human resource departments. They have to find a way to handle the deluge. Lots of students try it, but applying for jobs when you don't understand the qualifications is a total waste of time. And don't try to game the system. This isn't like a sophomore English paper where you can throw in a bunch of fancy terms and get a "B" out of it. Misrepresenting yourself on your resume by using keywords that don't reflect your real skills and experience will only get you rejected in the end.

2. Read each job description to understand what the company wants. Creating an ATS-friendly resume isn't just a matter of throwing in a bunch of key words helter-skelter. Jon Ciampi, CEO of Preptel, says that what matters most is the uniqueness of key words or key word phrases in a job posting. For example, many postings may list "strong organizational skills," but the healthcare coordinator position you're interested in also lists "abstracting medical records" as a key activity. As a rule, key words listed first in a job description are the most critical and the ones you should match in your resume if you have that capability.

If you find all this "keyword talk" a little overwhelming, Preptel has a cool tool that will analyze how your resume would be scored by an ATS for a specific job. Located at www.Preptel.com, the product is called Resumeter. It has kind of quirky interface, but it's free to use and can readily show you why your resume could get zapped when you apply for that dream job. Best of all, Resumeter suggests ways to reformat your resume so you will be a stronger candidate. To learn more, check out this video about Resumeter at http://bit.ly/10GeFDr. Or go to Preptel's website, create an account, and upload your resume for analysis.

3. Include key words from specific job postings in your job or internship listings whenever possible. That is where an ATS will score them highest. You also can add a paragraph near the top of your resume labeled "summary" or "profile." This section should summarize key skills and areas of expertise that match the requirements of the job description and language from the organization's website. One technique advocated by John Wilpers, founder of Degrees2Dreams.com, is to create a "word cloud" using a generator like Wordle.net (for PCs) or TagCrowd.com. Go to your potential employer's website and copy text from the job description, as well as Web pages describing their mission, strategy, culture, and values. Paste this text into the word cloud generator and create a visual image of the words and phrases most important to your target employer. Work as many of these key words as appropriate into your profile or objectives section. This should improve your chances of being flagged by an ATS. Here's a key word cloud showing frequency of word use generated from the Apple.com/jobs/us/corporate website describing the company.

administrative **apple** applications business communications **corporate** creative **customer** design **development** **engineering** estate **experience** expertise field **finance** hardware human information iphone legal locations looking **management** **marketing** merchandising network **online** operations organization people **products** project provide real resources **retail sales** service skills **software** strategically **support** systems talented **teams technology** user world worldwide

4. Follow a strict format when organizing your resume. Always start with the former employer's name, then your title (e.g., marketing intern), then the dates you were in the position. An ATS always looks for the company name first. Never start work experience with dates. That just confuses the computer.

5. Always use the label "professional experience" to describe internships and jobs. You won't stand out by getting creative with terms like "Career Achievements" or "Professional Development." In fact, the computer is more likely to skip over your experience completely if you don't label it this way.

6. Include all skills and capabilities used in every job, internship, or volunteer position. For example, if you worked with Excel spreadsheets for six months in one internship and for six months in another part-time job, list it in both places. Otherwise, you don't get credit for the total experience you have with that capability. If you just list Excel as a capability or skill at the bottom of your resume, the ATS won't give you credit because it can't attach a time frame to it. Employers are looking for people with X years of experience in certain skill sets. You must include specific skills for each position you held to get credit for those skills.

7. Always include your address on your resume. Resume expert Karen Siwak says Zip Code is often one of the first screening parameters used by hiring managers. If it's not present, your resume gets a low score. Don't put contact information in the header or the footer because the computer doesn't read those areas.

8. Never send a resume as a PDF document (unless *specifically* requested), and don't include graphics, pictures, or logos. A PDF too easily confuses an ATS, and any graphical elements will mess up the ATS interpretation of the text. When writing your resume, just stick with Microsoft Word, if you can. That's the software least likely to confuse an ATS, and your resume is more apt to be scored accurately.

9. Don't obsess about beating the system. Even if you think you're a perfect match for the job, the odds are you will never hear back from the company when you apply, given the volume of applicants, unless you have a personal connection there. One recent study found only 10% of companies reply to every applicant. Don't get emotionally attached to any particular opportunity when you're applying cold. You're just setting yourself up for discouragement. Experts advise you're still much better off putting that energy into networking.

Applicant Tracking Systems are one of the most dramatic—and frustrating—changes in the job-search process. And many career counselors don't understand that yet. Getting past an ATS makes finding a job more of a lottery. This is one technology that really works against you if you don't understand it. Using these tips doesn't guarantee success, but they will definitely improve your chances of landing an interview.

Get LinkedIn or Get Left Out

When it comes to LinkedIn, the world's largest professional network, you are in one of three places. Either you've never heard of it, you know about it but aren't using it, or you've created an account and don't use it much. There's lots to learn about LinkedIn and it can be overwhelming. This section will show you how to start getting benefits quickly. And if you are already using it, jump to the tips on how to accelerate your job search with LinkedIn.

What happens when you meet someone you like at a party, and they admit they don't have a Facebook page? Pretty strange, right? That's how most potential employers will view you today if you aren't on LinkedIn. You must be there to be taken seriously as a job seeker in most fields.

Here's the experience of Taylor, a psychology major from the University of Illinois:

I have a lot of classmates who wished they knew sooner how to really use LinkedIn. It's a great tool if you start using it early in your search. I started following big companies around Chicago on LinkedIn, so my home page would show me any job openings they had. I learned about the companies and types of positions that existed. It also really helped build my network. I would look at whom my connections were connected with. For example, say a friend a year older than me was connected to a marketing firm where I wanted an internship. Then I'd ask her if she knew that person well enough to introduce me.

Five quick steps for starting on LinkedIn

How do you get on LinkedIn? It can be intimidating. Begin with the five steps here or see "Build Your LinkedIn Expertise" for more detailed information.

1. Create a key-word rich, detailed profile. When you join LinkedIn (and why not join…it's free!), the first thing to do is complete your profile. Think of this as the "Common App" for your job search, except you won't be submitting it to schools. Potential employers will be using it to check you out. A good profile makes you findable. To look professional pay particular attention to:

Your Photo—Get a head-and-shoulders shot. Dress in business casual attire, or better. Nothing silly or social.

Your Headline—This is the first thing anyone sees when you come up in a LinkedIn search so make it meaningful. Think of it as a slogan telling the world who you are. "UCLA senior seeking aerospace marketing position." Or "Financial analyst intern at Fidelity Investments." Or "Junior/English Major, Wake Forest."

Your Summary—Definitely include key words related to the field or types of jobs you want to pursue. Make this concise and readable. See the sample in Exhibit 13-2.

Your Work Experience—Copy and paste material for this section from your resume, but elaborate: add more activities, skills, and accomplishments; use relevant key words where appropriate.

Your Status—This is not Facebook, so every update here must be totally professional. Once you start building your network with LinkedIn, try to post relevant updates at least weekly. Is there an article or blog post you want to share? Did you attend a career fair? Have an interesting interview? Tell your network about it so your ongoing job search stays on their radar.

Exhibit 13-2: A LinkedIn Page to Learn From

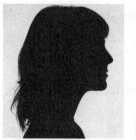

Carmen Trudell
1st

Marketing Assistant at Gigabuy Media
Greater Boston City Area | Public Relations and Communications

Previous   London Clicks, Asimov Associates

Education   Boston University

[Send a message ▾]

274
connections

BACKGROUND

  SUMMARY

Specialties: Online Marketing: e-mail, SEO (link building, keyword search and analysis) social media strategy and analytics, content creation and distribution (blogging/forums/podcast)

Consumer Public Relations: building media relationships, brand awareness and identity, full PR campaign development, social media management, PR writing (press releases/media kits/media alerts/op-eds/newsletters)

EXPERIENCE

Marketing Assistant
Gigabuy Media
May 2012 – Present (11 months) | Boston, MA

Drive affiliate and email marketing campaigns to increase SEO, content marketing and public relations goals for leading travel startup backed by TripAdvisor, the world's largest travel site.

Manage all social accounts, increasing Twitter daily gains by 75% and Facebook discussions by 30% to date.

Content marketing efforts resulted in features and interviews from Bloomberg, Amateur Traveler, and Huffington Post.

Social Media Intern
London Clicks
February 2012 – May 2012 (4 months) | London, UK

Managed major social accounts for leading PR agency, named New Medial Agency of the Year.

Generated analytics and created social content for airlines bmi and bmibaby helping to produce an award-winning visual campaign with over 60,000 shared photos named "My Europe."

Built relationships with beauty bloggers to increase brand buzz as primary community manager for Ministry of Cosmetics.

Consumer Food/Retail Intern

Asimov Associates

September 2011 – January 2012 (5 months) | Boston, MA

Created media lists, researched potential for- and non-profit partners, wrote press releases and pitches for major clients Baskin-Robbins, Dots, Bailey's and Dave & Buster's.

▾ 1 recommendation

Wendy Sanchez
Account Executive at Neptune Communications

Carmen was one of the brightest and most focued interns I have managed during my time at Asimov Associates. The Entire Consumer Food/Retail team valued Carmen as an important member of our team because of her dependability and understanding of...View↓

Build Your LinkedIn Expertise

Learn more about LinkedIn tools and features:

- Go to www.learn.linkedin.com

- View www.patrickomalley.com/linkedin-quick-start-tutorial.html

- Read *How to Find a Job on LinkedIn, Facebook, Twitter and Google+* by Brad and Debra Schepp, McGraw-Hill, 2012.

2. Connect with your existing network. Once you have a decent profile on LinkedIn, start inviting people to join your network. LinkedIn will ask you to provide access to your email address book. This is a good place to start, but you certainly won't want to invite everyone into this new professional network.

Focus on your older, more serious friends who are likely to be making connections of their own as they start their careers. Don't forget professors, as well as former bosses, colleagues from internships and volunteer organizations, and any career counselors you've worked with. Now make a list of people you know outside of school: your parents' friends and neighbors, classmates' parents, people from church, anyone with whom you have a direct or indirect connection. Consider inviting them to join your LinkedIn network. And from now on, anytime you meet someone during your job search who might be helpful, invite them to connect with you on LinkedIn. (Of course, some older folks and nonbusiness-oriented friends won't be on LinkedIn or have a profile and never check it. But this group is becoming smaller.)

When you invite people to connect, *always* customize the message in a sentence or two. (LinkedIn lets you do this.) It can be as basic as "I found your ideas very helpful when we talked, and I'd like to stay in touch." If possible, suggest some way you might be helpful to them. Never, ever just send the default message "I'd like to add you to my professional network." That just says, "I'm lazy" and "I don't really care about you."

3. Research companies and fields. As a senior at the University of Illinois, Taylor used LinkedIn to research a group of companies in Chicago identified as "best places to work." This helped her learn more about firms where she might want to work and the types of jobs she would be interested in. LinkedIn allows you to search companies by industry, location, and size. It also shows employees already part of your network who could provide you with more information for your search and maybe even some introductions. Start "following" companies you're interested in through LinkedIn to get regular updates on job postings, new hires, departures, and products.

4. Build out your network. Your LinkedIn connections should continually grow and one of the easiest ways to do that is to tap into your school's alumni network. Here's how Carl used LinkedIn after graduating from Colorado College.

I was living in Minneapolis after graduating, but wanted to expand my search to San Francisco. So I started using LinkedIn to search for CC grads in the city and see where they worked. If it was a financial firm, then I'd search their company and figure out where they were in the chain of command. Then I'd read their profile and shoot them an email.

LinkedIn is effectively replacing alumni databases in many schools because it provides more up-to-date, relevant networking information for job seekers. Like Oregon State, Caltech, or DePaul University, your school probably has an active alumni network on LinkedIn. Join it today.

5. Start searching for jobs. Steps 1-4 are essential because you must have a strong presence on LinkedIn before you hunt for specific jobs. If a potential employer looks you up on LinkedIn, which they will, and finds a half-assed profile, no photo, and three connections, they're not going to take you seriously. There's too much competition to take this lightly.

One of the cool things about LinkedIn, however, is that it shows you job postings tied to the content in your profile. You also can create an email list to be notified when more jobs like these are posted. Want to broaden your search to other types of jobs in other geographic areas? Use the "Advanced Search" feature in the upper right of the screen.

LinkedIn's job-search engine immediately shows who in your network has ties at the company posting the job. Now you can ask people you already know for personal introductions to learn more about the organization and the job. LinkedIn even allows you to connect directly to the company's website to apply for a particular job, using information from your profile.

Advanced search: now maximize LinkedIn

Here are three things that you can do with LinkedIn to enhance your job search.

1. Join LinkedIn groups. Take advantage of its extensive use of business-oriented groups. Once you have a profile, access the Groups Directory at the top of your LinkedIn homepage. Here you will find groups that LinkedIn suggests might be of interest. Obvious ones will be school alumni groups and groups of young professionals in your region. Also search for other groups that might be worth exploring. Read about each group's purpose to see if you want to join. Don't be scared off if the group appears closed. Unless it is for a membership-only organization, if you apply politely and explain your interests you will usually be invited to join.

Be sure to scroll down to the bottom of any group listing to see other related groups that might be of interest. Once you join a LinkedIn group, you have access to all its members, even if you are not directly connected to them. You also have access to a special jobs section, if the group has one. As a group member your role is to listen, learn, and contribute whatever you can to ongoing discussion threads. Networking like this is first about helping others as much as possible. Once you do that people will be glad to help you in return.

2. Ask for recommendations. Potential employers view LinkedIn recommendations as a form of pre-interview reference checks, and they can greatly enhance your image as a job candidate. Try to get at least one recommendation on your LinkedIn profile for each internship, job, or volunteer position you have held. It's easy to ask bosses and colleagues for recommendations, using the email form available under the "profile" tab at the top of the screen.

LinkedIn recommendations are an increasingly popular proxy for references and every one you have makes you a stronger job candidate. Since you're in the job market, you want recommendations to highlight the key attributes hiring managers are looking for. Thus, when asking someone for this reference, it is important to customize your request so it includes specific details about what you want mentioned. For example, *"If you could provide a brief recommendation about my recent internship as a lion tamer, it would be great if you could mention how I saved your life when…"*

3. Use LinkedIn constantly to support your networking and research. Don't treat LinkedIn as a static Web page you create once and then ignore. Your profile and network should be continually evolving. (See the Special Section at the end of the book to learn how Carmen, a Boston University public relations major, constantly updates her profile to increase her visibility with potential employers.)

Experiment with the Advanced Search capabilities in the upper-right corner of your profile page. This way you'll become much more effective at identifying companies of interest and people you wish to connect with. Want to work in an art gallery in Atlanta? (Good luck paying off those college loans!) Enter keyword "galleries," select "arts and crafts" under industry, and enter an Atlanta Zip Code. Bang! There are 121 people you might contact.

LinkedIn offers premium accounts for job seekers, which can make it much easier to reach out to people you don't know. Those extra job-search benefits start at $20 per month. It might be worth trying for a few months to increase your visibility to employers and your ability to connect with people outside your network.

Like all technologies, LinkedIn will evolve and its perceived value among users will change. Do you remember MySpace? Some longtime users are complaining that LinkedIn is becoming overrun with recruiters and, as with Facebook, there have been some privacy problems. But for now it is a fantastic resource for young job seekers. You are greatly handicapping yourself if you don't take advantage of it.

Answers to Job Search Technology IQ Quiz

Give yourself one point for each "Yes" answer. If you scored 7 or above, you're doing well, but there are still important things you don't know about using technology to find a job that will prolong your job search. If you scored 4-6, you're average but have a lot to learn. If you scored less than 4 on this quiz, you must be the parent of a new grad!

Checklist for Action:
Master Applicant Tracking and LinkedIn

___ 1.Take the Technology IQ Quiz to make your technology gaps explicit. Awareness of your real knowledge level about the technologies central to your job search is essential for setting priorities and learning what you need to know.

___2. Find someone who really understands ATS and ask them to critique the format of your resume. This might be a counselor in your school's career center, but more likely it will be a recruiter at a career fair or a family friend whose job in a medium-sized or large company involves hiring people.

___3. Revise your resume to conform to ATS requirements outlined in this chapter. (See Chapter 15 for more on resumes.)

___4. If you don't have one, create a LinkedIn account today and start filling out your profile. Set a realistic goal for yourself of when you will complete the profile. The closer you are to graduation the more critical it is. If you're already out of school, getting a decent profile on LinkedIn is a top priority.

___5. Join your school's LinkedIn alumni group immediately. Use LinkedIn's advanced search capabilities to identify alums from your school working in professions and geographic locations that interest you. Use the script in Chapter 12 to ask people for informational interviews.

CHAPTER FOURTEEN

Using Social Media Tactics to Get a Job

Do the math: there are a lot more job seekers than jobs. Sure, you'll have recruiters banging on your door if you're a primary care physician, a nuclear engineer, or a mobile apps developer. The rest of us are competing for a shrinking universe of high-skilled jobs. To win, you'll need every advantage you can get. That's why you've got to use new technologies to launch, not limit, your career.

Chapter 13 described two applications—Applicant Tracking Systems (ATS) and LinkedIn—you need to be in the game today. This chapter details other technologies that will make you a stronger candidate. It shows how to:

- Avoid three mistakes that can kill your job search.

- Use social media applications to increase your visibility and credibility with potential employers and take your networking to a new level.

Three Technology Traps to Avoid

1. Avoid "Monster" time wasters in online job hunting

One of the most consistent themes in my research with recent grads is how frustrating and demoralizing it is to use big online job boards. Monster.com and CareerBuilder.com were singled out as particular time wasters when students started their job search by spraying generic resumes out to employers for any opening that appeared interesting. Madison, a psychology major at the University of Michigan, expressed a common sentiment saying:

At first, I would feel productive when I spent an entire day searching for jobs using those websites, writing applications and cover letters. But then I'd get no response, so I'd put all this work in for nothing. It felt like I was sending applications to nowhere.

An undisciplined online job search through big job boards is a trap. You are applying for jobs that hundreds, or even thousands of other people are competing for. You also are probably applying to a bunch of jobs at once, which means your resume can't be customized enough to make it through the ATS discussed in Chapter 13. In fact, the odds are a human being won't even read your resume. At first, you feel virtuous because at least you're *trying* to get a job. ("Hey, Mom, I applied for ten jobs today!") In reality, you're wasting time when you could be doing something much more productive, like tanning on the frat-house roof.

This isn't to say all online job boards are bad. Niche industry boards like Idealist.com (for nonprofits), environmentaljobs.com, and greatinsurancejobs.com are more likely to be productive. It's still a long shot though if you don't have a personal contact in the company, and if you haven't done enough research to customize your resume. Don't be seduced into undisciplined online job searches. The keys are focus, contacts, and customization.

2. Don't let your "digital footprint" keep you unemployed

According to a recent study, more than 90% of hiring managers will check you out on the Internet, looking at Facebook, LinkedIn, Twitter, etc. to see how you portray yourself online. And more than 70% of employers say they have turned down job applicants because of what they found when researching the candidate online. The most common reason applicants are rejected: lying about their qualifications. These discrepancies will show up in your LinkedIn profile. So make sure it's aligned with your resume.

Other reasons employers will reject you after a quick Google search include:

- Inappropriate photos
- Posted content about using drugs
- Posted negative comments about a previous employer
- Demonstrated poor communication skills
- Spelling and grammar mistakes

All kinds of things can kill your chances of landing a job if you don't carefully manage your online image. Rule #1: Google yourself and find everything others might see that would influence their opinion of you. Don't overlook those unflattering spring-break photos on your friend's Facebook page. Ask your friend to remove them.

How to Clean Up Your Act

After deleting anything questionable from Facebook, Gen-Y jobs expert Pete Leibman recommends setting your Facebook page to "private" and using a respectable public profile photo. Even then, assume everything on your Facebook page can be viewed by anyone. You don't know which of your 1,000 Facebook friends was an intern with your prospective employer and could provide access. As a final step, have some older friends Google you, too, and provide their feedback on posts or tweets that potentially can hurt you later. Don't give employers a reason to disqualify you. If you're still nervous, www.reppler.com offers a service that analyzes your social networking accounts to identify inappropriate content that will tarnish your online image.

3. Failing to do your research before a job or informational interview

One small company CEO starts every interview asking the job applicant if he or she visited the company's website. If the answer is "no," he ends the interview right there. The availability of information online has raised expectations tremendously for potential employers and even professionals you meet with for career advice. You can't show up to an interview today without knowing about the company and the people you are talking to. Everyone knows the information is available, and they expect you to review it and come to the meeting with *intelligent* questions about the organization and the role you might play there.

An example of how research pays off came from Lily, an art history major from University of California, Santa Barbara. Seeking a position in high-tech marketing, she applied for an "online ad trafficker" position for an educational website. The CEO emailed back that she should come in for an interview that day and be able to speak about the ad trafficking process she would use. Lily recalls how she frantically prepared for the interview:

> *I literally knew nothing about ad trafficking. I started to panic because I wasn't finding the exact phrasing on the Internet that the CEO had used. Finally, I found a blog out of the UK that described the process. So I created flashcards and memorized them and repeated what I had just learned during the interview. If I hadn't found that one blog that explained things, I never would have gotten the job. I couldn't answer all their questions, but it was clear I had done my research.*

Failing to do adequate online research is a trap job seekers easily fall into, and it can make all the difference in winning or losing an opportunity.

The lessons from these three technology traps are:

- Focus on productive job-search activities. Don't waste time on big Internet job boards.

- Clean up and monitor your online image. Don't let a stupid photo or Facebook post keep you from getting a job.

- Always be prepared for your interviews. Employers know there's lots of information online about them. Don't embarrass yourself by not using it.

Tweet Your Way to a Paycheck

Carmen, a public relations major at Boston University, got two interviews that led to job offers, in large part because she used Twitter before attending her first job fair. (See Carmen's story in the Special Section for more details.)

Zoey, a recreation major at Central Michigan University, attended a national conference of meeting planners where she started seeing the power of Twitter in her job search. "Someone began following me after the conference. Then one day she contacted me via Twitter with a job opportunity."

You may already be using Twitter to share ideas about music, movies, and food. But Twitter is also an essential resource for job seekers in many fields. It can alert you to job opportunities, increase your visibility to potential employers, and educate you about the industry you are trying to break into. Twitter can be a great asset when used in collaboration with blogging, which will be discussed later.

A lot of people don't "get" Twitter, including your parents, probably. When you first jump in it can seem disorienting and super-ficial. Who can say anything useful in 140 characters, right? Who cares what you think? It turns out a lot of people do.

145

Here's the bottom line. Millions of professionals now use this social media application and in some fields like marketing, graphic design, and journalism it is a job requirement. Whether you continue to tweet once you're employed will depend on your profession and your company, but it can help you get in the door.

Setting up Twitter for a job search

For a job seeker, Twitter is somewhere between LinkedIn and Facebook in terms of formality. You can combine something of your professional aspirations and personal interests, e.g., "love marketing and food." Getting started with Twitter is easy. Open an account at Twitter.com. Complete your profile carefully because first impressions are very important. Space is everything when it comes to tweeting, so choose a Twitter handle or username that isn't too long and includes some part of your name. Part of the strategy here is to build your personal brand. (For more on branding, see Chapter 15.)

Assuming you don't have your own Web page, include the URL to your LinkedIn account when creating your profile. Including your location also will increase how often you show up in searches. After setting up your account, Twitter gives you the option of scanning your email address book to identify your contacts already using this application. It's your choice whom you "follow," but the goal is to broaden your network and use Twitter to become more visible in professional circles so you can get hired. You're not trying to recreate your list of Facebook friends.

Twitter will suggest people or organizations you might want to follow. The tweets of those you decide to follow flow into your Twitter stream to view each time you log in. There are several ways to figure out whom to follow. Check out websites like Twellow.com and Listorious.com to identify experts and organizations you can learn from. Or enter search terms on your Twitter homepage, such as "Maryland healthcare" or "Idaho banking" to get an idea of who is tweeting on these topics. Touching the photo on individual tweets that come up will show you the tweeter's profile, and you can then decide if they are worth following.

It definitely takes time to appreciate the power behind direct messages, retweets, and hashtags. As you get more facile with Twitter, you can learn how to do even more, like connect with websites that provide continual feeds of targeted job postings in your region. Like online job boards, however, these postings are seen by many people, so not only do you need to respond fast, but you also must do additional research to customize your application and look for any personal connections to give you an inside track on the position. Here are two Twitter-based services to check out:

TweetMyJobs.com—Combines job hunting with social networking by connecting your Facebook and Twitter profiles. You can specify highly targeted job offerings, which you can receive via Twitter, phone, or email.

TwitJobSearch.com—An easy-to-use basic search engine for jobs posted on Twitter.

Twitter isn't for everyone, and it can't replace face-to-face meetings and an internship experience. But if you are willing to jump in and be temporarily overwhelmed, it is a great way to accelerate your networking and learning about different fields and companies. There's one other thing you can do to make Twitter an even more powerful asset.

Blogging to be Different

Okay, you've done all the right things. You've spent your semester abroad. You've had some good internships. You've even done impressive volunteer work off campus. Your grades are pretty good and you've decided what kind of job you want. But how does a hiring manager differentiate you from the one million-plus other graduates entering the job market? Frankly, everyone looks the same.

How can you stand out to be sure you end up in the 50% of recent grads who have good jobs? Start and sustain a blog.

A blog, as you probably know, is a website where items (insights, observations, stories, etc.) are posted on a regular basis with the latest entry appearing first. Blogs are often authored by an individual and include a mix of text, images, and links to other websites. They usually have a theme or specific topic.

> *Jarred Taylor started a blog while a student at Davidson University majoring in political science and French. His blog, which was linked to his resume, didn't have lots of readers, but Google hired him into its legal department because they recognized that a student with the commitment to write regularly and articulately about topics of interest had the skills needed to thrive at the company. Jarred recalls, "Everyone who interviewed me from the recruiter to the phone screen to the senior attorneys during the videoconference, asked me about the blog. 'What do you blog about? Why? Give an example of something you've learned from what you've researched.'" Jarred has since returned to law school, but continues to blog. Read about his exploits, including his elaborate marriage proposal, at jarredtaylor.com.*

Blogging gives you a chance to do three critical things, but only if you blog about a niche topic in the industry you want to join:

1. Prove you have the skill sets you claim in your resume.

2. Show you have industry knowledge and are familiar with industry issues.

3. Connect with key industry players not as a weak job applicant, but as an industry professional interviewing those players about important topics.

Your blog demonstrates your skills as a writer and a critical thinker. It is also a chance to communicate your passion and humor.

Lots of students start blogs today. It's easy to get started. For advice and instructions to launch a successful blog, check out:

- En.support.WordPress.com/get-started/
- www.problogger.net/
- Buy *How to Write Great Blog Posts That Engage Readers* by Steve Scott for $1 on Amazon. A good investment!

The *only* problem with good blogs is that most people don't keep them going. That's how you can stand out. Here are five keys to using a blog as a key asset in your job search:

1. Post regularly. Blogs with only a handful of posts are useless. In an ideal world you will post weekly, but you need to add new material at least monthly.

2. Show off your writing skills. If you think and write clearly blogging is a great showcase for your talents. You can be irreverent, passionate, and personal but don't be crass or mean. Your future boss is reading this!

3. Focus on a topic related to your future work or field of interest. In practice, most student blogs end up being reflections on college life. If they are well written and thoughtful, that's okay. But the real power of a blog comes when it focuses on issues of interest to potential employers. "The hardest thing is coming up with a good topic," says John Wilpers of Degrees2Dreams.com. You need a niche. For example, a student in Southern California blogging about food in Los Angeles is too broad. A blog about "Thai food in L.A." makes more sense.

4. Use your blog to meet industry leaders. One real payoff from blogging is it gives you an excuse to contact people you'd like to meet. When doing research for a blog post, it's reasonable to contact leaders in your target industry for a brief in-person interview. Ideally, develop blog topics to put you in touch with people who you'd like to speak with for an informational interview, says Wilpers.

For example, if you wanted to work in sports management for the Washington Redskins, you might start a blog about the best sports marketing gurus in the Washington area, approaching the thought leaders at D.C. marketing agencies (including those working with the Redskins) and interview them about sports marketing best practices. Or say you want to work for an environmental agency in Los Angeles. Start a blog about the best coastal protection efforts in southern California, and interview the key players, including the thought leaders (who also might be the hiring managers) at agencies where you'd like to work.

The point is writing a blog gives you a reason to talk to the experts in the career field you want to enter. In the process of asking questions and becoming smarter about issues in this profession, you become a more visible and attractive job candidate. Then you can call them back three to six months after your interview, and ask what they are hearing about job opportunities in the area. Once you have interviewed them for your blog, Wilpers cautions, "You never, ever violate the relationship by asking them directly for a job."

5. Increase your visibility by linking to other social media. Before heading to her first career fair in New York City, Carmen, a PR major at Boston University, put up a blog post discussing the event with details about the companies that would be there. Of course, in reality not many people are reading Carmen's blog. That is, until she tweets about her blog post, with the hashtag used by the career fair. This means everyone checking out the event on Twitter now knows about the blog post, including the companies at the fair. This led directly to a couple of interviews and internship offers.

Connecting your blog with other social media platforms (e.g., Twitter, LinkedIn, and Facebook) can significantly increase the visibility of your posts. This type of extra content helps separate you from the pack, which is key in a highly competitive job market.

Oops! Almost Forgot Facebook

You're already an expert on Facebook. Not much to learn there, right? Well, maybe you don't know what a useful role it can play in your job search. The bad news is not one of my 30 successful grads said, "Facebook was key to my job search." In fact, here's what they said:

>—*"I made myself unsearchable. You never know what could rub someone the wrong way."*
>—*"I was careful what I put on Facebook, grooming my profile so I didn't shoot myself in the foot."*
>—*"I changed my last name and email on Facebook so no one could find me."*

In reality, Facebook will play a relatively minor role in your post-college career, but that doesn't mean you should abandon it totally. You've got hundreds of "friends" on there and you can take advantage of that. Aside from cleaning up your profile, here are three things to do to make sure Facebook is working for you.

1. Turn your profile into a job-search asset.

Make sure the information on your Facebook page helps you look like a good potential employee. That's the advice from Brad and Debra Schepp, coauthors of *How to Find a Job on LinkedIn, Facebook, Twitter & Google+*. This means:

A. Fill in education and work sections completely under "Edit profile." If you had any practical courses related to your career interests, add them, too.

B. In the "About you" section of your profile, create an elevator pitch that will appeal to potential employers by answering the question, "What do you do?" For example, "Looking to use my organization and communication skills to help sales teams soar" or "Want to apply my talents for collaboration and creativity to support faster product development in a high-tech setting."

Think of your Facebook page not as something that will keep you from being hired. Treat it, instead, as a billboard that shows you off as a great candidate. Think of it as a temporary strategy while you are in the job market.

Be more intentional about what you paste on your wall. This means posting links to interesting articles you've read or, better yet, blog posts you've written. Mentioning news about interesting projects you've worked on, blurbs about books you've read, movies, or TED talks you liked. When in doubt, favor more positive posts. Venting about people and stupid politicians doesn't enhance your image as a potential new colleague at work. You don't have to look like an aspiring priest or nun. Fun photos of socializing are still fine. Recent research actually shows partying photos can lead a student to be positively judged as friendly and extroverted. But just be smart about it. You are trying to boost your stock as a smart, creative, and fun colleague.

Finally, occasionally use your "Status Update" to let people know you are on the market, but not in a needy—"I'm unemployed"—way. Try something like:

—*"Exploring opportunities to work in healthcare marketing where I can really make a difference."*
—*"Looking to start a career in financial services after graduation."*
—*"Excited about an interview with the CIA tomorrow."*

2. Start building relationships with potential employers on Facebook fan pages.

"Like" companies you are interested in to begin getting news updates. Look for opportunities to make interesting comments about something an organization posted on its Facebook page. It's great to show you can add value to an online community, says Miriam Salpeter, author of *Social Networking for Career Success.*

When you identify target companies or get an interview set up, often you will have no connection in your LinkedIn network. Try using Facebook to connect casually with people who might help your job candidacy or provide more information about the company and how to break in. With a search on Facebook you can identify employees who work there and contact them with a polite note asking for help.

3. Look for job postings on Facebook

Company pages will sometimes include job postings, but remember the limitations discussed earlier about applying without a personal connection. One productive way to use job postings on Facebook is with the app, BranchOut. When you sign up at BranchOut.com, you create a new professional profile separate from your personal information on Facebook. Use this app to look for postings at a specific company and you can find out which of your Facebook friends and the friends of your friends work there. Then, just like LinkedIn, you can start using your personal network to learn more about the company and the job opportunity. It always comes back to who you know and the quality of your relationships.

Even when you have technology working for you in your job search, increasing your visibility and credibility and creating opportunities for interviews, you still have to sell yourself. Resumes and interviews have never been more important because the market is extremely competitive. How do you make sure you close the deal when a great opportunity arises? These questions will be answered in Chapters 15 and 16.

Checklist for Action:
Make Social Media an Asset, Not an Adversary

___1. If you are "spraying and paying," STOP IT NOW!! That is, stop responding to job postings on major online job boards with your standard resume. There are much more fun ways to waste your time.

___2. Google yourself, using variations on your name to see your digital footprint. Wherever you can, but particularly on Facebook, remove inappropriate photos, comments, and posts that a potential employer could judge negatively. Ask an older friend or parent to review your online image and to suggest changes. Make sure your Facebook privacy settings limit access as much as possible.

___3. Set up a Twitter account and start following some companies, experts, or groups related to jobs you are interested in.

___4. Consider whether blogging is a good strategy to support your job search. If so, identify a relatively narrow topic to focus on and start developing a list of topics you can write about.

Sell Yourself

Translate your experiences into skills employers care about.

CHAPTER FIFTEEN

How to Write a Resume That Rocks

Working on your resume is about as appealing as "hitting yourself in the head with a hammer." So says career expert Martin Yate, who quickly adds, "Yet owning a killer resume is the foundation of every successful job search." That's the dilemma. There are lots of reasons to postpone writing your resume, but you won't make serious progress in your job search until you have a good one. This chapter shows what really matters in creating your resume, how to avoid costly mistakes, and where to find great resources to save you time producing a resume that works for you.

Ask the Experts

There are plenty of resources available—career counselors, books, Internet templates—but you should expect lots of conflicting advice on what makes a good resume. One humanities major recalls:

> I'm don't think the career counselors who reviewed my resume had worked much with liberal arts resumes. They would critique it, but then I'd read those online articles about how to write a great resume, and there was lots of conflicting advice. So I asked my Dad, who runs a small business, to tell me which resumes looked best to him. He said there's no absolute right way to do it. After a while, grad school was looking like the easy way out of this mess!

Looking for advice in books or online? Sure, there are some excellent resources, but most are mediocre at best. Narrow your focus by weeding out anything published before 2008; things have simply changed too much in the hiring process since then. (See "Resume Writing Resources to Check Out.")

The problem with many books, says one resume expert, is they deal only with people who have a great background. What's missing is advice for the poor schlub with a 2.5 GPA who needs it more than most.

Resume Writing Resources to Check Out

There are many books and Internet resources to help you create and revise your resume. Only use ones updated since 2008. Older resources won't be sensitive to the requirements of Applicant Tracking Systems.

1. *Résumé 101: A Student and Recent-Grad Guide to Crafting Résumés and Cover Letters that Land Jobs* by Quentin Schultze, 2012. This is one of the best guides out there. It's concise with a clear process for creating resumes and cover letters based on the author's experiences working with hundreds of students.

2. *Best Resumes for College Students and New Grads*, 3rd Ed., by Louise Kursmark, 2012. An excellent book with a clear process to help those with limited work experience create an effective resume.

3. *Résumé Magic: Trade Secrets of a Professional Resume Writer*, 4th Ed., by Susan Britton Whitcomb, 2010. This book contains everything you need to know about resume writing, and more. In fact, it will be overload for some people. Look for a copy in your library or career center.

4. *Knock'em Dead Resumes*, 10th Ed., by Martin Yate. Offers a more sophisticated and entertaining approach to resume writing. It is useful if you know what kind of job you want.

5. Here are a few online sites offering helpful information:
   http://www.rileyguide.com/resprep.html
   http://degrees2dreams.com/blog/category/resume-help/
   http://www.job-hunt.org/resumes/
   http://www.quintcareers.com/resres.html

Do it Yourself

One reason it's so hard to create a killer resume today is because of how they're actually used to evaluate your qualifications. Not only does this summary of your capabilities have to survive the automated Applicant Tracking Systems (ATS) described in Chapter 13, but if a person looks at your resume, it is only for three seconds before it lands in the "maybe" folder or, more likely, in the trash. So you're trying to create something to quickly separate you from the pack and make an immediate impression. Here are four strategies for producing a resume to help you stand out:

1. Focus on your resume's REAL objective. The purpose of a resume is not to get you a job. It's to get an interview. You want to get in the door so you can sell yourself. Career development rock star Richard Bolles points out that employers use resumes mostly to see if there is a reason to screen you out. And it doesn't take much:

—*One or two typos (forget it!)*
—*Not enough demonstrated experience*
—*Awkward formatting*
—*Lack of relevant skills*

Include any of the above and you're out of the running. Period. Your goal is to create an easy-to-read, grammatically perfect document highlighting only those skills and accomplishments most relevant to a particular job opening. It should not be a testament to how great you are. This summary document must communicate how you can meet and also exceed the employer's expectations, so they'll want to learn more.

You might create a general generic resume to start, but be sure to tweak it every time you apply for a different type of position, or to a particular company or industry.

2. Focus on translating your relevant experiences into skills, knowledge, traits and, most importantly, results the employer will value. For college grads with limited work experience this is the most challenging and important task in creating a winning resume. Create an exhaustive list of experiences and accomplishments that demonstrate capabilities you may not even recognize you have. Then translate this raw list into relevant, valuable, and valid skills, along with knowledge and traits written in language employers will understand. This will become the core content of your resume.

Don't try to do this without some guidance. Visit your school's career center to see if they have an easy-to-follow process for translating experiences into valuable capabilities. However, be careful. There is a good chance your school's career counselors are still operating on outdated premises, so take some of their advice with a grain of salt. Another option is to spend $10 to download a book such as Quentin Schultze's *Résumé 101*, which will walk you through the process. I'll bet your parents will even spring for this. Schultze advises: "The basic question you want to ask yourself is what your life experience has taught you about the big three—your skills, knowledge, and personal traits."

3. Format for consistency and readability. Resume layout is critically important. First, unless you are only applying to small organizations, format it to meet the demands of the ATS described earlier. If your resume can't pass this test, then you might as well not have one. (Revisit the section in Chapter 13 for tips on creating an ATS-friendly resume.)

Resumes today should lead with a position-focused summary or profile statement that provides an overview of your skills, knowledge, and traits directly relevant to the job for which you are applying. These replace more traditional objective statements, which tell the hiring manager what kind of job you want and how excited you'd be to learn new skills. I've got news for you. They don't care! Crazy-busy managers only want to know one thing. Will your capabilities help them meet their needs?

Why Personal Branding is so Important

You're likely to hear a lot about "personal branding" when you start trying to sell yourself. This concept is an important way of thinking about how you can differentiate yourself from other job seekers. And in such a competitive job market, finding positive ways to stand out is essential.

Think of your personal brand as the overall perception interviewers and potential employers have of you. You can influence or develop your brand when you consistently communicate what is unique about you—your achievements, experiences, and attitude.

Your resume is one way to communicate your essential characteristics and values. Other factors that influence how hiring managers perceive you include your dress and appearance, how you interact with others, and your online presence as communicated on Facebook, LinkedIn, etc.

It's important to integrate your values with your accomplishments, and capabilities. Listing cool companies on your resume, but also posting toga-party photos on Facebook is not a wise brand-building strategy. Conflicting messages about who you really are raises questions about your credibility, and trust is central to every influential brand.

Check out these resources for more about how to use personal branding as a way of selling yourself more effectively:

- www.DanSchawbel.com—Considered the master of personal branding for Gen Ys, Dan's website has all kinds of tools to help.

- www.personalbrandingblog.com—Another personal branding blog started by Schawbel with lots of other contributors. An excellent resource.

Here are some examples of summary statements from *Résumé 101.*

—*"A resourceful administrative professional seeks to serve a local nonprofit to ensure cost-effective operations and increased fundraising opportunities."*

—*"New media production graduate with cutting-edge software skills seeks to serve an advertising agency in a team-oriented environment where excellence is valued."*

—*"A conscientious, dependable economist with strong interpersonal skills and extensive database abilities desires to serve a governmental agency's consumer affairs division."*

Each of these summaries would have been customized for a particular job posting and, where possible, descriptions used would match key words in the specific posting.

Getting the formatting of your resume right is an ongoing process. You will get lots of advice from well-meaning people, and you will have to ignore some of it. For example, counselors in your career center may advise listing "education" above your "work experience," because the latter is probably limited. Forget it. Unless you're applying for an academic job, your "experience" must come first. That's what employers care about today.

The best advice on formatting your resume is available from people familiar with the requirements of an ATS and who do the hiring in your fields of interest. Listen closely anytime you can get a recruiter or hiring manager to give you feedback on how your resume is laid out. Even if you're not talking about a specific job, be proactive and ask hiring experts for feedback on your resume's layout and content. For more quick advice on how to format a resume that won't die in an ATS, read the Degrees2Dreams blog post, *"9 Steps to a Resume That Avoids Black Holes"* by Krista Scozzari at http://bit.ly/VBGFpD.

4. Customize, customize, customize your resume. One of the most painful lessons learned by the successful grads I interviewed is they wasted an incredible amount of time sending out generic resumes in response to online job postings. They call it "spraying and praying." Don't do it! You're much better off watching another episode of "The Bachelor" or playing Grand Theft Auto. At least you'll enjoy wasting your time. Resumes are only effective if you submit ones targeted to specific job openings. There are three reasons why customizing your resume for particular positions is so important.

First, employers today won't spend any time guessing whether you have the skills and traits they're looking for. They have no patience for figuring out how your recent internship or history degree helped you develop the critical thinking and communication skills they need. You must make that translation and connection for them, depending on the specific requirements of each job.

Second, tailoring your resume for each job is essential because the hiring process is so heavily dependent on keyword matching. I can't emphasize this enough. *If the language in your resume doesn't match up with keywords in a particular job posting, you will not get the interview.*

And third, customization today increasingly means having a graphic or multimedia resume that will help you stand out from the crowd. These are controversial among career counselors, and they'll freak out human resource managers in, for example, government agencies, law firms, or financial management companies. (HR types and lawyers worry about charges of discrimination in hiring.) But if you're applying for a creative, highly innovative or entrepreneurial position, then definitely consider creating a graphic resume that could include your photo in a professional setting, two QR codes linking to a brief video of you talking about your skills and interest in the industry.

A second QR code could link to a video of your best reference talking about what a great employee you'd be. Alternately, link to a website showcasing a portfolio of your work. Remember, an ATS does not read anything but text. If graphic elements show up in a resume fed into an ATS, it becomes electronic trash. How do you solve this problem? Always send two resumes and label the documents: "[Your Name] Resume (Graphical)" and "[Your Name] Resume (ATS-friendly)."

If you create a resume with graphics, have a back-up that is "ATS-friendly." That means text only. Resume expert John Wilpers advises, "Always indicate in your cover letter that you have attached two resumes, one with graphics, including a photo, and one that is a graphics-free, ATS-friendly resume." This allows the company to use the one they prefer. For more ideas about graphics resources, see Wilpers' blog post, *"How-to: Great Student Resumes in 5 Steps"* at http://bit.ly/V8HjtV.

How to Use Cover Letters to Your Advantage

Like it or not, career services directors and employers say the quality of writing among college students has deteriorated significantly. As a result, says one career center director, "More and more companies are saying they just don't want to read cover letters because they can be so painful. The quality of your letter can be a huge factor, good or bad, in your application." This means you can turn cover letters to your advantage if you follow these tips.

Always submit a cover letter, unless explicitly instructed not to. Research on the success rate of online job applications shows that failure to include a cover letter leads employers to assume the candidate is not really serious about the position.

Personalize every cover letter, but remain emotionally balanced. Never use a standardized emotionally detached, or a one-sentence letter ("Attached please find my resume."). On the other hand, you don't want to be overly emotional or unprofessional ("I'd be so excited to work at your company!"). Strive for balance that communicates sincere professional interest and enthusiasm for a specific position.

Use the cover letter to put a positive spin on your resume. This note, which should be less than one page, is a legitimate chance to sell yourself. Ideally, your cover letter should include:

—A specific statement about the particular position you're applying for.
—Mention of any personal connection you have to the company, if you're sure that person would speak highly of your application. (e.g., Don't mention that ex-boyfriend who works there.)
—A clear statement of why you're interested in the position and highlight particular skills qualifying you for the job. Use your resume's summary statement as a starting point for linking your capabilities to the job.
—A brief reference that demonstrates you've done some research, know something about the company, and have put thought into your decision to apply.
—Address the letter to a specific person and department, if at all possible.

Treat every cover letter as a writing sample. Because employers are skeptical about the communication skills of many young grads today, this is your chance to stand out. A professional, well-written cover letter can set you apart from the flood of resumes a hiring manager must review. Get help drafting these, at least initially. Get feedback on drafts from your school's career or writing center or from your parents. Proofreading cover letters and resumes is a great task for your parents. Grammatical mistakes and typos will kill you with potential employers. The more eyes that review your documents before submitting them, the better. At the very least, read it aloud. That way you'll hear things your eyes don't pick up because you've read it too many times. Awkward writing will jump out at you when you hear what you wrote.

Examine cover letter samples for quicker drafts. Unlike resumes, there's a lot more agreement about what makes a good cover letter. Explore the resources in your career center, or go online to find advice on drafting good letters. Boston College, for example, has a good resource page on cover letters at http://bit.ly/W8auP2. Check out the video and written samples.

Selling yourself to any potential employer is a multistep process. An excellent resume and cover letter are key to getting in the door. Then you've got to convince the hiring manager you're the right person for the job. The next chapter shows essential steps for nailing the job interview, which is critical to getting an offer. Job interviews are a high-stakes game you must be prepared to win!

Checklist for Action:
Enhance Your Resume

___1. **Go to your career center or buy a recent book like** *Résumé 101* **to get a good process for translating your experiences into marketable skills.** Don't assume every career counselor can do this well.

___2. **Ask anyone advising you about your resume, "Do you think my resume is set up well for an ATS?"** If you hear any hesitation in their answer, be very cautious about what advice you take from them because they don't understand how resumes are processed by medium-sized and large organizations today.

___3. **Ask at least three people who read a lot of resumes in their job to critique yours for readability and formatting.** This could be a recruiter at a job fair, a family friend, or a veteran career counselor. Expect to get conflicting advice. Make the changes that make the most sense to you.

___4. **Develop files on your computer to keep various versions of your resumes and cover letters to use when applying for different jobs.** Adapting these will save lots of time when applying for positions in the future.

___5. **Find someone you trust to proofread your resume and cover letters.** Avoiding typos and grammatical errors will keep you from being rejected for unnecessary reasons. (This can be a good job for your parents.)

CHAPTER SIXTEEN

How to Nail Your Job Interview

You may have a fantastic resume, great contacts, and terrific job prospects, too. That doesn't mean you'll get the job. No matter how good you are, you've still got to nail the interview.

Companies hate making hiring mistakes and the competition for most positions is intense, so chances are you're going to have more job interviews than you ever imagined. And these will be demanding, high-stakes meetings. Here are four keys to successful job interviews.

1. Preparation is everything.

When your parents went on a job interview at your age, they just showed up in a clean shirt ready to answer the proverbial query, "So, why do you want to work here?" The interviewer described the job and the company, not expecting the applicant to know much about both. Maybe it was a little stressful, but it wasn't complicated. That's all changed. Today, employers expect you to know:

- All about their organization and something about the industry they're in.

- Whatever you can learn about the job itself from the job description and other sources.

- How the skills and traits in your resume make you a good candidate for the position.

An economics major looking for a job in finance learned the hard way what happens when you don't do your homework:

The interviewer asked what kind of investment research I had done. So I started talking about individual securities, and I could see the reaction on her face. This company didn't invest in individual securities. I should have known that.

There are many places to get information about a company, its industry, and the specific job you're interviewing for: the company's website, Google news, LinkedIn, company blogs, Facebook, Twitter, and websites of competing companies. For quick advice on how to do better research in preparation for your interview, see the links on your school's career center website, or view sites like Boston College's resources on interview prep at http://bit.ly/V3NZud.

Also, don't overlook www.Glassdoor.com, a site that provides an insider's view of more than 200,000 companies and includes interview questions. If you know who will be interviewing you, definitely learn about his or her position, career, and education on LinkedIn. They will most certainly be looking you up there.

One thing to set you apart from other applicants is to be sure you've read several articles relevant to the company and industry where you're interviewing. Scan major business publications such as *Fast Company, Forbes, Fortune, The Wall Street Journal, The New York Times business section,* or *Business Week.* When Ethan was graduating from Beloit College, he was surprised at how he impressed interviewers for a major insurance company when he casually referred to a Forbes article he had read. They offered him a job.

According to a recent study in *Forbes* (See, aren't you impressed?), hiring managers are skeptical about the research skills of today's college grads. So, you can immediately set yourself apart from the competition by being well prepared.

2. Explain how the capabilities and traits on your resume match job requirements.

In addition to researching the company and job, a critical piece of preparation is thinking through how your experience and education makes you an excellent candidate for this job. This is where a lot of new grads fail. Matt Berndt of TheCampusCareerCoach.com says:

When interviewing for an internship or a job, you must realize employers don't inherently "get" you. Just because you majored in journalism, you can't assume a potential employer knows the breadth and scope of your training in journalism. You must be ready to have conversations that show why you're relevant and qualified.

Being prepared to convince an interviewer you are right for the job involves several steps. First, know your resume cold. That means what skills you've used and your accomplishments in every job, internship, or volunteer experience listed. You can't sound hesitant when an interviewer asks you what was the biggest challenge you overcame on the project you did during last year's internship.

Second, analyze the requirements and qualifications listed in the job description of the position you're applying for. Most important, you must practice telling stories and anecdotes that clearly demonstrate how your past performance proves you can handle the job.

Here's a neat tool for linking your experiences to the job requirements. Sara Pacelle heads NorthBridge Career Partners, a career advisory firm that works with college students and new grads. She advises clients to use her firm's tool called a "Career Credit Chart" for each position they're applying for. (See Exhibit 16-1 on the following page.) This is a two-column form where in the left column you list every requirement and qualification mentioned in the job description of any job you're applying for.

Then, in the right-hand column, opposite each job requirement, write accomplishments and experiences you can describe in brief examples to demonstrate you have the necessary qualifications. For example, if the job posting calls for "advanced Excel skills," you might list your "bank internship credit card project" as a reminder to talk about that experience to demonstrate your strong Excel capabilities.

Exhibit 16-1

Career Credit Chart™
Interview Prep Tool

Job Title: Entry Level Financial Analyst
Company: Compass Finance

Position Qualifications and Requirements (from Job Description)	Your Accomplishments and Experience (craft stories around each)
1. BA Economics, Finance or Accounting	• BA Economics GPA 3.6 • Dean's List 4 semesters • Relevant Coursework
2. Demonstrated excellent Math and Excel programming skills	• SAT Math 790 • Won Math award in high school • Paid math tutor • Completed Excel programming class
3. Financial services internship or other prior finance work experience	• Summer 2012 Internship with Morgan Stanley as financial analyst
4. Leadership and teamwork skills	• Captain of Varsity volleyball team • Resident Assistant in dorm • Formed rock band
5. Confidence and Entrepreneurial spirit	• Went abroad junior year to Egypt and now import rare Egyptian goods and manage an online marketplace on Ebay. Secured participating investors.

Used with permission of NorthBridge Career Partners

In some cases you won't have a specific work-related story to tell. Then, you'll have to reflect on other aspects of your life that illustrate an important competence. Maybe you resolved difficult conflicts in your sorority, played a leadership role on a sports team, coordinated events for your church youth group, developed documentation as part of a thesis project, or managed a project for an on-campus group. No matter what the source of your story is, be prepared to elaborate on how and why you took the actions you did. Whenever possible, use words that describe outputs or accomplishments. For example, "I... analyzed, coordinated, delivered, evaluated, obtained, organized, researched, or trained."

Ending interviews is one of the trickier moments in your search for work, but it is also an opportunity to leave a lasting impression if you use tricks suggested by John Wilpers, founder of Degrees2Dreams.com. When the interviewer says, "That's it for me. Do you have any questions?" do one of two things. Refer to a short list of questions that show you researched the company to identify recent developments or challenges it's facing.

Alternatively, you can end with a story that reflects on your past achievements relevant to the job opening. You could say, "No I don't have any questions, but we didn't discuss something I think illustrates how suited I am to help you meet your needs. May I tell you about a time I...." Wilpers points out stories are more memorable than facts and will end your interview on a positive note.

3. Practice, practice, practice interviewing.

Career expert Ron Fry says, "What constantly surprises many interviewers about first-time job seekers is how unprepared they are. ... Too many inexperienced job seekers think they can just 'wing it.'...." The days of winging it to get a serious post-college job are long gone. One advantage to having lots of interviews during your job search is they provide a natural form of practice. But only if you learn from them, as Yong's story demonstrates in the Special Section at the end of the book.

There are many ways to practice for upcoming interviews. Here are some of the most effective. First, get a list of the most common and challenging interview questions from your school's career center or the Internet. This list almost always starts with the proverbial request to "Tell me about yourself." It is essential to think through and even write your answers to questions you are bound to get, such as: What are your greatest strengths? Weaknesses? Where do you want to be in five years? Why are you interested in this position?

There's a good chance your school offers mock interview sessions that are a great opportunity to practice and get feedback. Also check out other resources to support your practice needs that your career center provides.

Another option is to have a friend videotape you answering mock interview questions. Are you fidgeting too much, touching your hair, using "like" or "um" every fourth word, not making eye contact? This direct feedback is painful to watch, but powerful in helping you improve fast.

Finally, do you have a trusted family friend with business experience you may have spoken to for an informational interview? (See Chapter 12.) If so, ask this person to interview you for a job posting you're interested in. Provide him or her with a list of some questions you want to practice answering. Ask for frank feedback on how you did.

One unexpected benefit of a lengthy job search is you will undoubtedly improve your interviewing skills. When Taylor was graduating from the University of Illinois with a B.A. in psychology, she applied for several jobs where she was a marginal candidate just to get the interviewing experience. This definitely helps. But you will become more competent if you also practice and learn from the feedback you receive along the way.

4. Be prepared to nail a remote interview.

Busy managers need to narrow down the field of finalists quickly, and will often use technology to do this. But Skype and phone interviews come with their own set of pitfalls. To make it to the next round, you need to know what works and what doesn't.

And don't be surprised if you end up conducting phone interviews in all kinds of unusual places. Laura, the Lehigh University journalism major, found herself doing a key last-round interview in the Café Car on an Amtrak train. Heading home after a full day of meetings, she says, "I had lost my voice because I had done so many interviews. My voice is squeaking as I'm struggling to be heard on the train and people are yelling at me. It was terrible."

Phone interviews can catch you off-guard in unexpected ways, as Brooke discovered after graduating from University of California, Berkeley. This sociology major got a phone message after submitting her resume to an online entertainment website. She recalls:

When I called back, I didn't realize the call was going to be my phone interview. I wasn't prepared. I didn't even have the job ad in front of me. I was really flustered. The editor asked what was most interesting about the job posting. I know I sounded like a kid.

You will probably do a ton of phone interviews during your job search. Here are some tips to make them more successful.

Schedule the interview when you can be prepared. If a potential employer calls and wants to interview you, don't let this person pressure you into talking when you're not ready. Say you're busy at the moment, e.g., in a meeting, late for class, etc. Suggest a time that works better for you, even if it is just 30 minutes later. Schedule the call when you can be prepared and focused.

Make sure your cell phone signal is strong or use a landline. Try never to do a phone interview where reception is bad. You will be distracted and sound less confident.

Prepare as you would for an in-person interview. The difference is you can have your resume, the job posting, and other key materials in front of you because the interviewer can't see you. Be sure to have your questions and stories you want to use close at hand.

Listen carefully to the questions and *never* interrupt. Recruiters commonly complain about interruptions, which are seen as rude.

Focus on answering the interviewer's questions. Since the interviewer can't see your body language or be impressed by your cool new suit, the quality of your responses is extra important. You will do most of the talking, but don't ramble on too long, which is easy to do if you're nervous. After talking for a minute, cut your response short. You can always ask, "Would more detail be helpful?"

Remember, tone is key. You want to sound confident and friendly, even if you're incredibly nervous. Smile while you talk. You will sound more energized and confident if you stand up and pace a little. Let your personality show. It's ok to admit you're excited, nervous, or curious to learn more about the job opportunity. But show you've done your homework and always keep the conversation professional.

Be sure to ask about the next step in the process. Inquire if there is anything else you can do to help the interviewer. Phone interviews are an important part of your job search, so you need to be prepared.

Skype interviews

Online video interviews, usually via Skype, create new opportunities and risks for young job seekers. One recent study found that more than 40% of companies now use video interviews as part of the hiring process. To ace your Skype interview, remember the following tips.

Look professional. Not only do you need to dress as you would for an in-person job interview, but your Skype presence also must be professional. If your Skype name is "gatorgal" or "spartanstud," change it if you expect to get a grown-up job. Your profile picture is just as important. You don't want the interviewer to see anything that signals you're not ready for prime time.

You're on stage. Clean up the area behind you visible on camera. Make sure whatever the interviewer sees in the background is neat and not distracting, particularly if you're in that sorry space you call your bedroom.

Make sure the lighting is flattering. You want your face well lit from the front, either by a window or a lamp above the computer monitor. Ensure there's no window or light on behind your head, or your backlit face will look like Darth Vader. Lighting is tricky in a video interview. See the web video "How to Look Good on a Webcam" by photographer Matthew Rolston.

Check your technical connections. You don't want your interview interrupted by a sketchy computer connection, so test your set up by practicing a call to a friend or family member. This confirms your technical set up and allows you to warm up a little and see how you look and sound.

Look at the interviewer. Making good eye contact is a big challenge in video interviews. Instead of looking at the screen, train yourself to look into the camera, which is almost always on the top edge of your monitor. When staring at that little round camera be aware of your facial expressions when listening to the interviewer. Without real eye contact it's like watching TV. It's easy for your face to go blank or glum. Practice listening with a smile.

Continually engage your interviewer. In face-to-face meetings, it's impolite to appear distracted by other things. But on Skype, if you start droning on, you're interviewer is likely to begin checking his or her email or headlines on CNN. Your job is to engage this individual with animated, enthusiastic, and clearly well-prepared responses.

Online video interviews are a great way to save time and travel, but to stand out from the competition you must pay close attention to other important factors so you get invited to the next round. The video "How to Ace a Job Interview on Skype" at Time.com will coach you on doing your best.

Don't forget to say "thank you."

A considerable number of recent grads I studied found themselves interviewing candidates for internships and jobs within months of taking on their new roles. One thing that consistently surprised these new interviewers was how many applicants did *not* bother to send thank-you notes after the interview. Several commented that thank-you emails or, even better, handwritten notes, could really help a candidate stand out.

Your thank-you note is another opportunity to remind the interviewer how you can add value to the organization. Refer to details from your interview. Mention several specific ways you can contribute to the organization if you get the job. While these notes are a good way to make yourself memorable to those doing the hiring, make sure the memories you create are positive. That means watching your grammar and spelling very carefully. Brooke, a University of California, Berkeley grad, learned this lesson after interviewing with the editor-in-chief of an online entertainment website.

> *Of course, I emailed them a thank-you note. But the worst feeling was hitting the "send" button on the email and immediately realizing I had spelled the word "editorial" wrong in the subject line! I was kicking myself. Here I am applying for an editorial position, and I spell a word wrong because I was in a hurry. I didn't get that job.*

All written communication to a potential employer must be proofread diligently. Don't let typos and grammatical mistakes give hiring managers an easy excuse to eliminate you from a job you might love.

Some of the most memorable stories from your job search will probably come from the interviews you do—both good and terrible. See the Special Section for the stories of two guys with intense interviewing experiences that you can learn from. The next chapter shows how to get the most out of your school's career services office.

Checklist for Action:
How to Nail Your Interviews

___1. Next time you have an interview spend an hour reviewing the company's website, searching Google News for recent articles on the organization, and Glassdoor.com for any insider information.

___2. Get a list of common interview questions from your career center or see the Forbes article *"How to Ace the 50 Most Common Interview Questions"* at http://onforb.es/Y8c8wl. Write out answers to the questions you feel most uncomfortable answering.

___3. Next time you are going to interview for a job use the two column Job Description/Accomplishments Exercise described in this chapter. Identify your most impressive relevant experiences and capabilities that relate to the specific requirements listed in the job posting. Be prepared to provide examples demonstrating your skills and knowledge in action.

___4. Find out when your school's career center offers mock interview sessions to build your interviewing skills and get feedback on what you need to improve.

___5. The next time you have a phone interview, prepare as you would for an in-person interview. Schedule it at a time when you can be ready and make sure you have a strong phone connection.

___6. Dress for an in-person meeting, and pay special attention to lighting when you are asked to do a Skype interview. Watch the videos mentioned in the chapter for more specific coaching on how to prepare for an online video interview.

Ask For Help

Your best allies in your job search are closer than you think.

CHAPTER SEVENTEEN

What Your Career Counselor Won't Tell You

As a political science major at Penn State, Daniel dreamed of attending law school. He did well in school, but his board scores were low and pursuing his law degree meant going deep into debt. Also, because he worked continually to pay tuition, Daniel couldn't do the resume-building internships others had. He remembers visiting the university's career services office for advice:

I didn't want to give up on law school, but I was too intimidated to talk to a counselor. I just slipped by the secretary, picked up some brochures and skipped out the back door. Later I found out about career services workshops, which weren't as intimidating to me as one-on-one meetings. I wished I'd attended these seminars earlier to learn how to market myself.

Some colleges and universities are investing more in their career centers today to meet the increasingly complex needs of their students. Others, unfortunately, have suffered from budget cuts due to the Great Recession, just as their student caseload expanded. But even schools with a reputation for excellent career services—University of Texas at Austin, Clemson, Penn State, New York University, Keuka College, University of Oregon, Bentley University, and the Rochester Institute of Technology—can't satisfy everyone looking for help.

Whether you attend a small college or a large university, this chapter shows how to maximize your school's career development and job-search resources. It also provides some secrets career counselors won't tell you that might help you get a job faster.

Barriers to Using Career Services

Here are the most common reasons students don't take advantage of their career center.

1. "I don't even know what services the school provides." You're bombarded with scores of promotional offers from school organizations and academic departments, so it's understandable why info from your career center gets lost in the white noise of all the announcements. If you care about your life after college, those notices deserve more attention. This is particularly true if you are in a liberal arts program at a big university.

2. "I heard our career services suck." On some campuses this notoriety may be well deserved. "There are still appallingly too many educational institutions that don't care about career outcomes," says one prominent career services director. Before you decide that your school's resources are a waste of time, do check them out yourself. Don't take the word of a couple of students. They may be unprepared to do the homework needed or are unreceptive to the advice they received.

3. "I went to one career fair and it was lame." You won't solve all your job-search problems at one job fair. And working with career counselors also is an ongoing process. Things don't always start out smoothly. One student found his school's alumni database full of outdated addresses and gave up in a huff when a slew of emails were returned as undeliverable. But a year later he returned to career services and got some excellent networking help that led directly to a job.

You don't stop taking classes because of one bad professor. Your career center might be mediocre in resume coaching, but it might have a killer program in mock interviews or alumni networking. Don't give up right away. If you have a disappointing meeting with a career counselor, find another one you can click with.

4. "I want to do this on my own." Some students are organized and proactive enough that they don't need help from career services. That's fine. About 10% of those interviewed didn't use their university resources at all. But they often had close relationships with professors who provided coaching and advice. That's another resource you can tap.

How Will Career Services Look at You?

Experienced career counselors try not to judge students up front, but human nature makes it hard not to categorize students looking for job-search support. Career services staff is committed to helping you no matter where you are in your journey. One veteran career services leader summarizes it: "About 20 percent of our students totally get it, another 20 percent are out of touch or don't care, and the rest we can help succeed."

Good counselors take the attitude, "You are where you are today, and let's go from here." They work hard not to make you feel bad about past decisions or inaction. Still, knowing which group you fall into can make this interaction more productive.

1. *"On top of it."* These are the students who come to career services second-semester freshman year and apologize for getting a late start. By junior year, they've already had a couple of jobs or internships. They attend career fairs and networking events early in their college careers, and work on selling themselves in practice interviews. Counselors know these students

just need some reassurance that they are on the right track and they'll be fine.

2. *"Too focused and over confident."* These students have a short list of companies they plan to work for and, probably, an unrealistic idea of how careers unfold in their target industry. They may also have an unrealistic idea of how they stack up against the competition, considering their experience, industry knowledge, and performance in school. Students in this group are likely to dismiss advice from career counselors until they experience enough rejection firsthand.

3. *"Clueless about their job search."* If you're motivated and willing to learn, these students get the most help from career services. This is a logical place for many underclassmen to begin. As long as you start learning about career options and the job-search process by junior year, there's still time to catch up.

4. *"Unmotivated and uninterested in a career."* Counselors are continually surprised by the significant percentage of students who don't really care about pursuing work after college. Students in this group can't be helped by career services until they recognize that they have to own their job search. Nobody is going to do it for them.

Three Ways to Maximize Career Services

1. Be clear about what your career center can— and can't—do.

A career center cannot get you a job. That's up to you. But it can do more than you think. One savvy career services director says:

Students make the mistake of thinking the career center is only good for resume critiques. In reality, we may know where jobs are. We know the networks you could tap and conferences you could attend. Think of us as career strategists. A student can walk in here saying, "I have no idea what to do with my life," and an hour later, they feel much better because they leave with a plan to get started.

Even if you are a graduate, find out what services your career center offers. Knowing what's available can minimize the time you waste when you start your search.

2. Take advantage of special networking opportunities.

"I can't tell you the number of networking opportunities I share with students that are never followed up on," laments one career-center director. This is a lost opportunity because at no other time in your life will you have access to so many potential employers who visit your school in hopes of recruiting young talent. Career fairs, industry panels, networking dinners, employer information seminars, are all unprecedented opportunities to learn about professions, industries, and to connect personally with potential employers. Even if you are not interested in a particular employer, participating in these sessions will deepen your understanding of career options and help you narrow your focus.

3. Seek honest, constructive feedback on your strengths and weaknesses as a job candidate.

One veteran career services director describes a common scenario:

When some kids walk in the door I can tell they're a high-risk job candidate. They're not energized or reflective about what they want to do. And they have clear skill gaps. Either they're not a strong student, or their ability to present themselves well is limited, or they're not connecting with me. They're not in touch with what it takes to project themselves as someone who is bright, capable, and will get the job done. We can tell them what they need to do. Some people can take this type of coaching and some cannot.

If you're lucky, your career center can be a place to get honest—and sometimes painful—feedback about your strengths and weaknesses as a job candidate. But, as you will see in the next section, inviting constructive criticism can help improve your chances for success in the job market. It may be simple things like the way you dress for an interview or talk about your accomplishments. Or it may call for more difficult changes like the energy you project and your level of eye contact. Hearing this feedback is never easy, but it can be the greatest gift a career counselor can give you. Ask for it.

Of course, getting useful advice from career services assumes your school has experienced, well-trained counselors. Not every school passes this test, unfortunately. Ultimately, you have to decide if the resources available to you are useful.

Five Things Career Counselors Won't Tell You

There are always messages counselors want to convey but hold back for a variety of reasons. Becoming clued in now can be to your advantage and will help you get a job faster.

1. "Your job search is going to be a pain in the ass."

Why? Because it's going to require skills and behaviors you're unaccustomed to using, such as self-reflection and face-to-face networking with people you've never met. You're also going to have to deal with levels of rejection that you've never experienced. Getting into college was a piece of cake compared to the obstacles you'll have to overcome when competing for a good job. This is going to be harder than you think, but the good news is you'll get through it and learn a lot about yourself in the process.

2. "You'll be much more successful if you stop believing a bunch of stuff that just isn't true about getting a job."

Here are some assumptions that get students into trouble:

—*"The Internet is great. I can do this whole job search online."* Wrong. The Web changed the employment market dramatically, but the activities most likely to make you successful—face-to-face networking, strong interviewing skills, and challenging internships—have little to do with the Internet.

—*"English and anthropology majors don't get jobs."* Not true. Employers are looking for candidates who can demonstrate strong critical thinking coupled with strong communication and leadership skills. Demonstrate these attributes through extracurricular activities, internships, and interviews and your major is much less important.

—*"If I make the wrong decision about what job to go after now, I'll pay the price for years."* Baloney. The odds are you'll change jobs within two years anyway. And you're likely to end up in a different industry. The fluidity of today's economy makes assumptions about linear career development obsolete. Find an interesting opportunity where you will learn a lot and dive in.

3. "Our goal in counseling students is to make them a little anxious. We call it 'constructive anxiety.'"

Some students arrive at the career center totally panicked and paralyzed with fear. Others show up overconfident and unrealistic about the chances of landing a good job. Still others may be strong candidates, but they feel helpless about how to package and sell themselves. No matter what your emotional state is, good counselors want you to be a little anxious—not panicked—about your search. This increases the chances you'll listen and focus on what you need to do.

4. "Right now, you have a totally unrealistic idea of how people get into this industry." (Journalism, sports management, investment banking—take your pick.)

A lot of students dream of working in "cool" fields without understanding the dynamics of how careers evolve in that profession. For example, plenty of students graduate from the University of Texas at Austin thinking they can stay in the city and make a decent salary as a journalist. It doesn't work that way. Austin has one major daily newspaper, a few radio stations, and a highly educated population competing for the same positions. Matt Berndt of TheCampusCareerCoach.com, and former director of career services at the UT Austin College of Communication, explains:

> *Young people starting out in journalism typically begin in a small market and work for relatively low pay, like the farm system in baseball. To advance professionally as a journalist, you've got to move around. This means starting at the bottom and accepting that you'll have to move multiple times in your career. The question is, are you willing to make these sacrifices for your "dream career?"*

5. "I'm afraid to be candid with you because I don't want to hurt your feelings."

"Otherwise, I'd tell you: you need a shower, you're showing way too much cleavage, or your body language tells me you don't care about getting a job."

One highly respected career-services director confesses:

*We're so concerned about their self-esteem that we're terrified
of being candid with students based on what we observe—or
smell. We're being too diplomatic for their own good.*

Unless you invite a counselor to give you frank, constructive
feedback, assume this person is being diplomatic not telling you
things that will keep you from getting a job. This may make you
feel better, but it's not doing you any favors. You'll be successful
much faster if you invite experienced counselors to be honest about
your strengths and weaknesses for the jobs you are targeting. Of
course, like all advice, you'll have to decide what to listen to and
what to ignore.

Don't think like a "customer"

The high cost of college combined with a more difficult job
market puts much greater pressure on schools to help students launch
their careers successfully. Some schools invest heavily in career
services to provide students with a competitive advantage. Other
colleges are woefully out of touch with the changes needed. Regardless,
you want to get as much help as you can from your career center.

Like the varsity college athlete hoping to be drafted by the NBA
or NFL, the school and its coaches can help, but it's ultimately up to
the individual to make it happen. To land a great job, don't think of
yourself as a "customer" of career services. Yes, you have a right to
expect access to good career planning and job-search resources,
but access to these services is really all the school can give you. Getting
that good job is still up to you. One veteran career coach advises
students to think of their career center as a good friend who is really
smart and also has many great connections in your field. Isn't it foolish
not to take that friend's advice?

Of course, for better or worse, your parents probably will be a
key factor in your job search. Show them the next chapter to make
sure they are a big asset and not a distraction on your adventure.

Checklist for Action:
Tap into Career Counseling Services

Are you a second-semester senior? A first-semester sopho-more? A recent graduate? No matter what stage you're in review this list for actions to take now.

___ 1. If you haven't done this, find out *exactly* how your career center can help you. Check out the career services website to find out what specific services it provides. Then call or visit to get more details on how they can help you. Remember, you can't get it all by reading stuff on a website. And, even if you have graduated, the center may continue to provide alums with some services. Be proactive in educating yourself about how they can help: career counseling, aptitude testing, resume writing, practice interviews, job postings, alumni networking, career fairs, and more. One good question to ask: *How do students who are most successful at finding good jobs use career services?*

___2. Ask classmates, upperclassmen, and recent grads for referrals to career counselors who are really helpful. Like professors, some counselors are much better than others. Who are the hot ones? (No, not in that way!) Schedule appointments with them.

___3. Start attending career fairs and networking events as soon as you can. The more you learn about different careers and work environments, the more you'll know what you like and don't like. You'll also get ideas about where you might want to intern.

__4. Once you find a counselor you like, keep asking for feedback on what else you could do.** Share your job-search plan with them (or get the counselor to assist you in developing one) and invite their critique and advice. You may not like everything you hear, but it's valuable input.

CHAPTER EIGHTEEN

Why It Pays to Let Parents Help

Your parents are likely to have invested a lot in your college education—financially and emotionally—which explains why they are more than a little interested in what you're going to do with your degree. How do you coach them to be truly helpful in your job search, instead of a pain in the butt? *This chapter is actually written for your parents.* Ask them to read it, and then talk about how they can assist you.

There are many roles your parents can play. Here's what some recent grads said:

> —*In college you need to separate yourself from your parents, but I wouldn't have gotten my job without my Dad.*
> —*My Dad just said, "Get a job so I don't have to support you." But my Mom played a huge role. She was like a life coach.*
> —*My parents were incredibly supportive. They used all their connections to get me exposure to industries I was interested in.*
> —*My parents knew there wasn't much in the area for jobs so they encouraged me to leave home.*
> —*My Dad graduated from high school and my Mom got her GED, so they don't know what to say except "Keep trying."*

For Parents Only:
How to Support Your Kid's Job Search

Considering the investment you've made in your child's education, it's particularly painful to stand back and watch them flounder. How can you be supportive? Here are six suggestions. Some you can do immediately. Some you will never do. It all depends on your relationship with your child, his or her readiness to pursue a serious job hunt, accept advice from you, as well as your own work experience and parenting style. (See "The Parent Coach: What's Your Style?")

The Parent Coach: What's Your Style?

Mom and Dad's reaction to the challenges their child faces in today's job market reveals a variety of distinct parenting styles. Which one will you use? Your decision matters because some approaches are much more effective than others in helping your kid develop job search skills that will be essential in the long run.

Helicopter Parents go off the deep end and over involve themselves in their adult child's life. The media is full of stories of parents who show up at job interviews with their children and call potential employers berating them for not hiring their offspring. A more subtle version of this is parents who create resumes for their kids or who attend career fairs to collect literature for Johnny who is "too busy" to show up. These interventions undermine the new grad's efforts to develop these skills on their own.

Career Micro Managers use a high-control style that continually intervenes in their child's job search efforts and tries to sustain a sense of urgency. Well-intentioned parents are likely to take this approach when they see the challenges their kid faces. This approach can also backfire. One recent grad observes:

My parents are very actively involved in my life. My Dad is constantly asking questions and seeing where he can add his two cents. It's annoying when they're trying to run your life.

Woodstock Revivalists are parents who want to be understanding and let their child launch their own career. But when their young grad seems to be making no progress and rejects polite offers of help, patience and empathy can turn to anger and fear that this investment in a college degree was wasted. One psychology major recalls:

My parents never pushed me to figure out what I wanted to do, which was a blessing and a curse. Mom was kind of happy to have me home. She was pretty hands off, which was her way of making me independent. But it didn't make me feel any sense of urgency.

Another new grad had a different experience:

A few months after graduation, my parents started to panic. They were asking to look at my cover letters and resumes more often, which only made me an obstinate 23-year-old. I got more stressed out and pushed back.

Compassionate Coaches use an engaged, collaborative approach, if their child is open to it. This type of relationship involves helpful questions, challenging a young grad's assumptions, encouraging them to try new experiences, listening with empathy to their fears and frustrations, and letting them know the limits of family resources available to support them. Anna, a political science major from UCLA, described her parent's approach:

I was very anxious after graduation. I had a lot of talks with my parents. I didn't want to just get a job. I wanted to set myself up to go to a top public-health school in three years. My parents told me not to apply for jobs if they weren't going to help me in the long run. My mother pushed me to apply to places outside the Bay Area where I grew up. I was upset with her, but in the end, it was the best advice.

Outsourcing to Career Experts has become a solution for some parents who recognize they don't have the skills or patience to advise their children in how to get a job. (They may also decide the school's career center isn't doing enough.) A cottage industry has developed for career counselors who work almost exclusively with new college grads. This is definitely a viable option for parents who recognize that engaging an outside expert provides the best hope of quicker results for their child.

Be clear about your own biases

Psychotherapist Mary Jacobsen asserts that all parents have conscious or unconscious biases about the careers their children should pursue. These beliefs grow out of your own experience and dreams for yourself. Keeping these biases to yourself will make you less effective as a parent, she adds.

To encourage your child to follow their dreams, be conscious of the example you're setting in your own life. Jacobsen, author of *Hand-Me-Down Dreams: How Families Influence Our Career Paths*, says, "The biggest challenge for parents is to be aware if they are following some passion in their own lives. What are you communicating by example?" The father who has pursued a career as a corporate lawyer because it pays more, even as he complains about his lack of fulfillment, is sending different signals about career choices than a Mom who loves being a high-school English teacher and is paid considerably less.

In managing your own biases as a parent, try to become more mindful of the indirect messages coming through in your tone of voice, facial expressions, and body language. Do you become unhappy whenever your son talks about a career in social work? Do you fail to make eye contact with your daughter when she expresses an interest in international finance?

Also consider what is left unsaid in family conversations about work after college. Even if you never speak about your feelings, your nonverbal expressions telegraph your reactions to children. Jacobsen explains:

Something that is powerful enough not to be talked about, but that is emotionally tangible, signals extreme importance to your child. For example, parents who insist that a child should feel free to move anywhere after college may contradict that message by showing sorrow, anger, or hurt through tone of voice, pursing of the lips, or the lift of an eyebrow. If you don't talk about your mixed emotions, you may unintentionally cause confusion for your child, who detects your discomfort, but is not sure about its source.

One source of confusion may be the lifestyle you created that your child may or may not want to replicate. This can have a strong unspoken impact on the pressures they feel in choosing a career. Andrew, who grew up in a prosperous town near Boston, says, "The grander picture my parents painted for me is what they have created out of life—how they raised our family in a nice suburban home, and that's what I want to do. I'm constantly thinking by the time I'm 40 I should have these things."

Another issue is the fear many parents have that their child is falling behind their peers because it is taking them longer to finish school or find a job. In my interviews, at least 25% of "successful" grads took more than four years to complete their undergraduate degree. (Nationally, more than 40% of students who start four-year programs fail to finish within six years, but that's actually a bigger societal problem.) Research shows it is indeed normal to take more than four years to finish college, and there is an enormous variation in the paths to becoming a successful young adult. So stop comparing your child's job search and career progress to that annoyingly perfect Harvard pre-med student down the street. There are too many variables at play that will influence the outcome.

Another bias to be aware of is the career lobbying you do that is couched in terms of duty, genes, or destiny. As a parent, Jacobsen says, it's easy to put unintentional pressure on your child with comments like:

—*"You're bound to be a teacher like your grandfather Frank."*

—*"You've always had the makings of a lawyer; you were always so good at arguing."*

—*"Our family has a great legacy in nonprofit work."*

In a volatile job market and an era of rapidly changing career options, no one is predestined for a particular line of work. But statements like these send powerful signals about our expectations, even when delivered with a laugh.

Be encouraging

As a parent, you're never conscious of all the messages you're sending your children, but you can be intentionally supportive of their job search efforts. Here are three ways you can make sure your kid feels supported.

1. Be enthusiastic. Let them know you're excited about the real progress they're making. Sometimes you may have to point out milestones they overlook, such as completing a marketable resume or a solid LinkedIn profile, conducting several informational interviews, or getting a job offer—even if it's one they don't want. "My Dad was so excited for me when I sent my resume packages out to design firms," recalls Faith, a graphic designer. "He knew how hard I'd worked on them."

2. Be patient and empathetic. So much of the career planning and job-search process occurs online today that most of the work is invisible. As a parent, this makes it hard to judge what's actually getting accomplished. One grad looking for work in nonprofits recalls:

> *Sometimes my Mom didn't see all the hard work going into my search. When your parent is working and they come home and see you sitting on the couch and they ask, "What did you do today?" it's hard to explain there's no news. I wish she could have understood more.*

Even if you know your child created a solid resume and is doing the right things networking and targeting the right employers, it can take extra effort to stay positive. Try to be a calming force. A grad who went through a long search advises:

I was already really frustrated with the search and a lot of my conversations with my parents just added to that. I didn't need any other stress. But I also understood they were frustrated about me having such a hard time.

3. Be sensitive to rejection. Most Gen-Yers graduating from college haven't had to deal with much failure or rejection. These are kids who always got trophies no matter where they finished. Confronting the realities of the job market can be a brutal awakening, notes one small-school liberal arts grad:

College is deceiving. You're riding high for four years. Many professors are telling you you're doing great. But then you get thrown into the real world and you fail a lot.

As a parent, one way you can be most helpful is giving your child the understanding and time to deal with rejection. A young grad from a prestigious school recalls:

Sometimes I wished my Mom was more sensitive to the rejection and the toll it was taking. She didn't understand how inadequate I felt. I had gotten this amazing degree at an amazing university, and why can't I get a job? Both my brothers were in computer science and got jobs right away. Entering the job market with a psychology degree was a very different beast.

Helping your child deal with rejection means giving them time to process it. This can be difficult for a parent who is more detached and looking at a bigger picture. ("Okay, that opportunity didn't work out. What's next?") Here's how one young woman experienced her parents when a job offer she accepted was withdrawn:

When I told them the job offer was gone they wanted me to get on to Plan B. But I needed them to acknowledge losing that job was stressful and dramatic. I wanted someone to say, "It's terrible. You're going to have to move home."

Your kid's timetable is not yours. That's painfully obvious. What's less clear is understanding when you're dealing with a young adult who would benefit from an added sense of urgency or when it's better to recognize their emotional need to slow down.

Never stop asking good questions

Timing is everything when coaching your college student or recent grad. An important way you can help is by periodically asking career-related questions your child may not be thinking about. One career services director suggests:

> *At least once a semester, question your child's assumptions about the classes they're taking and the activities they're pursuing. Ask things like: "What questions do you have about your career that you expect your courses will answer? Why do you think you want to work in finance or journalism (or whatever)? What questions do you need to answer to clarify your interests in this field? Do you know what it's like to work in a high-tech marketing department? How can you use what you know so far to make choices about your courses in the coming year?"*

In some cases, you may be discussing decisions about what to major in. Luke started as a business major at Christopher Newport University, but switched to philosophy his sophomore year because of his growing interest in religion. While on a family vacation in his junior year, Luke's father convinced him to add economics as a second major. Unlike his initial business studies, economics was something Luke found intrinsically interesting. That turned out to be a good move. As he approached graduation, Luke was planning to start a masters program in religious studies when he was unexpectedly invited to apply for a plum job with the Federal Reserve Bank. (See the Special Section for the amazing end of Luke's story.) A surprising number of recent grads I interviewed had double majors or minors that proved very valuable in their job search.

In other instances, you may ask questions designed to lead to better decisions about internships, potential jobs to pursue, and whether or not to accept a specific offer. Your goal is to enable your child to make more thoughtful choices without being pushy or dictating outcomes.

If you're like many parents, you wish it were easier to tell the difference between offering helpful advice on the one hand, and trying to control your child's decision-making on the other. To gauge your motives, Jacobsen suggests this test: When you give your child advice on career planning or their job search, notice how you react when they don't accept your recommendation. If you're angry and frustrated, you were trying to tell them what to do. But if you're able to accept their decision peacefully and be supportive, whatever the outcome, then you're playing the appropriate role in parenting an emerging adult.

Discussing majors or other career plans can be a touchy subject in some families. If you get significant resistance when raising these issues, maybe you haven't clarified expectations about whether your tuition checks are an obligation on your part, an investment, a gift, or an entitlement. Explaining how you view your contribution to your kid's future and what, if anything, you expect in return (e.g., decent grades, a little career planning, etc.) is a conversation to have as early as possible.

Support networking any way you can

Helping them network and arranging informational interviews will often be the most tangible ways you can boost your child's job search, if he or she is open to it. You may not be connecting them directly to a potential job, but by opening the door to conversations with people in fields they're interested in, you can help them clarify their focus and educate them so they can sell themselves better. Lily, an art history major, recalls:

The biggest thing that helped me was having a variety of adults to talk to about their careers. My Dad said people want to talk about their jobs. So, if you have connections, tell people, "My daughter is interested in learning about this. Or she wants to learn how you got into your career." So it becomes more storytelling. My Dad's approach made people so open.

Try collaborating with your kid to come up with a list of family friends and connections in industries that they're looking into. You may have to encourage them to reach out to people, but there's a balancing act between being productively pushy and being overbearing. You won't always get it right. That conflict is evident in interviews like this one where a young grad says, "My Dad was so good at setting me up with people." Then moments later, he complains, "My Dad was annoying. Can't I just go one day without having a networking conversation?"

The balancing act of helping your child network depends on many factors, including his or her willingness to accept your suggestions for connecting, the apparent relevance of your contacts to their career interests, and your kid's priorities at the moment. Because your kid's timetable is not the same as yours, get used to the fact that they won't reach out to people as quickly as you think they should. This is very frustrating when you "just know" that a particular contact is key for your child. One well-organized new grad says:

The best thing parents can do is network for their kids in a way that is not overstepping boundaries for them. That means don't always pressure them by asking, "Are you looking for jobs?" They know they need a job. What helped with my parents is they sat down with me and said, "We want to be as involved as you want us to be."

Be careful helping with nuts and bolts

It is tempting to assist your child with job-search basics, like resumes, cover letters, interview preparation, and even what to wear. One savvy Mom who is a professional motivational speaker advised her daughter to dress in formal interview attire, only to hear back after one job fair, "Mom, no one's wearing a suit!"

Unless you are in a job where you do a lot of recruiting and hiring yourself, be cautious when offering help in these areas. As discussed in Chapters 13 and 15, the criteria and formatting for effective resumes has changed so much in recent years that the advice you offer is likely to be wrong!

Of course, you can help your child by proofreading their resume if they want you to, making sure they haven't overlooked some achievement or work experience worth including. But the best advice when it comes to formatting a resume is to encourage them to get help from someone with up-to-date expertise, and even to suggest getting a second or third opinion. Do what you can to make sure your child is getting valuable coaching on this.

Editing and proofreading cover letters and thank-you notes is another way you can help. Reminders about the value of hand-written thank you notes, or even thank-you emails, can't hurt. Several newly employed grads in my sample had already found themselves interviewing potential employees or interns. They were struck by how often candidates didn't follow up with thank-you notes and how sending them made other applicants stand out.

One other area where you might make a difference is in helping your child prepare for interviews. One economics major recalls:

My Dad is an executive, so I called him when preparing for an interview. He interviews a lot of people for his company and he went through what he looks for. We even talked about posture. And he reminded me to do my homework on the company.

Coaching your kid for interviews will depend on whether you have relevant experience in this area. If not, try to ensure your child is getting assistance with developing these skills.

Role players in the job-search drama

Parents are likely to play very different roles in supporting their children through a job search. A psychology major recalls how her parents helped:

> *Every time I had an interview in the city, my Dad would drive me, and we'd practice on the way. Other times, I'd call my Mom crying and saying, "This is so hard!" She felt sad because she knew how hard I was trying.*

One thing parents need to be aware of in today's tough job market is how emotional collusion can undermine your kid's job search. Many parents don't want their children moving back home after college, but a significant number are secretly glad when they do. One recent grad moved home and worked in a local store, until finding a job he wanted in a distant city. He recalls:

> *My mother didn't want me to leave home. Obviously, she wanted me to get a real job. But she would have been happy if I stayed at that store for another six months.*

Be aware of the explicit and implicit signals you're giving your child about living at home—and leaving home—after graduation. This is a complicated issue with many emotional and financial implications. The main concern should always be helping your new grad develop into a strong, independent adult.

Other family members can also play important roles in the job search process. Sometimes an older sibling will be more effective at delivering messages that won't be accepted from a parent. The daughter of one career counselor I interviewed had inappropriate partying photos on her Facebook page. She ignored her father's pleas that she remove the pictures when she started a job search. Her Dad finally turned to her older brother who convinced his sister to take the photos down. Another young grad recalls how her older brother played an important role.

> My brother was able to tell me more about what to expect because he was closer to the job market than my parents. He would also point out when I was applying for something that was unrealistic.

When family ties are strong, get the word out to all relatives who might be helpful in expanding your kid's network. If you have older children who have had some success in the job market, don't hesitate to draw on their experience in advising their younger sibling. Other family members, such as aunts and uncles, can also be an important asset, particularly in setting up informational interviews with people in distant cities where your child wants to relocate.

Know your limits

A clear majority of the students I interviewed described Mom and Dad as providing very important or even fantastic assistance in landing a good job after school. Another 25% indicated their parents played some role, usually in the form of moral support. Only about 10% of the "successful" grads I interviewed said their parents played little or no role in their initial job search. Where will you fall? Maybe your kid won't need any help, or maybe out of a growing sense of independence will loudly reject your offers of assistance. That's not a bad thing, although it may be frustrating, and even heart-breaking, to watch your child flounder as they try to begin their career.

Unfortunately, most young grads are ill-prepared for the extremely challenging job market they face. As parents, we over-scheduled our adolescents in sports and extracurricular activities, thus limiting opportunities to gain the valuable work experience employers now demand. We have also fed them a steady diet of technologies that discourage face-to-face interaction and the development of interpersonal communications skills critical for networking. In the process of raising Gen-Ys, many parents have also intentionally limited the obstacles their children must overcome, not realizing how this can undermine their persistence, industriousness, and grit, traits so essential in today's workplace.

Now your child faces the toughest job market experienced by college grads since the 1930s. And this is a market you don't really understand, which limits your ability to provide assistance. Still, there are many things you can do, as outlined in this chapter. But the hardest challenge you face may be accepting the things you can't do. If your kid is going to become an independent young adult capable of making good career choices and landing a string of good jobs, he or she needs to learn from experience what it takes to succeed. That's a challenge young grads must take on themselves. But no doubt, you will be there to cheer them on.

And one of the best ways to meet the challenges of launching a career today is to learn from peers who are just a couple of years ahead of you. What do these successful grads wish they had known before starting their job search? What would they have done differently? How can you profit from that wisdom? That's the focus of the next chapter.

A *Parent's* Checklist for Action

__1. Reflect on your own career dreams and the compromises you've made.** Have you been able to follow your passions? How are your own unfilled dreams likely to influence the advice you give to your child about his or her future? Discuss this with your spouse or partner.

__2. Talk with your kids about the lifestyle they've experienced growing up.** Do they want to replicate that? Do they want more financial resources? Or are they willing to live a simpler life? What are their dreams about where they might live? Do as much listening as possible.

__3. Be aware of any tendencies you have to talk about your child's career choices in terms of duty, genes, or destiny.** Nothing about career paths is predetermined in today's work world.

__4. Plan regular conversations to learn how you can be of assistance.** If your kid is a sophomore, you may touch base every three months to discuss choices about courses, internships, and summer jobs. If they're living at home after graduating, you could ask to be updated every week or two on progress being made in the search. These requests can be very emotional, but explain that being kept informed about progress will go a long way to reducing your own concerns. This will make you easier to live with.

__5. Engage other family members—siblings, aunts, uncles, cousins—who might be helpful in the search process,** particularly around networking and effective technology use.

By senior year, try to collaborate with your child to create a list of family and friends to contact for informational interviews.

___6. Help with resumes, cover letters, and interview preparation. Make sure your child is getting good coaching on these job search essentials, either at school or through other up-to-date resources. Offer to proofread materials.

___7. Try to be a "compassionate witness" to your child's career development. This means offering advice and realizing that most of the time it won't be used—and learning to live with that.

Happy Endings: Grads with Great Jobs

Do the right things and everything will work out.

CHAPTER NINETEEN

Lessons Learned: "What I Wish I Had Known"

his chapter shares critical, first-hand lessons learned by grads just a few years older than you who succeeded in landing an excellent job.

This isn't some career counselor or your parents talking.

This advice could be coming from your recent fraternity brother, teammate, or classmate. Just a couple of years ago, they were doing what you're doing now. So listen up. When asked what lessons they learned after going through their successful job search, or what they wished they had done differently, five messages became clear:

1. Networking is Everything.

Don't be afraid to contact people. If someone is a jerk to you, just ignore them and move on.

That's the advice of Lucas, a University of Texas grad, now a freelance television production assistant. Carl from Colorado College works in investment management. He learned this lesson the hard way.

If I were starting another job search today, I'd immediately open as many channels as I could. My mistake was focusing too much on one contact, when I should have reached out to alumni from my college and other connections much earlier.

Lee, a grad from the University of Ontario Institute of Technology, who went to work for Enterprise Rent-a-Car, was surprised at the incredible networking value his school friends provided:

It's not what you know. It's who you know. The biggest thing I took away from school was to be successful you need to network. My fraternity was the best thing that ever happened to me.

Daniel, a Penn State grad who now works at the U.S. Department of Justice, agrees:

Definitely tap into your alumni base. At PSU, people who you've never met will help you just because you're both alums. I didn't realize that. There are so many Penn Staters in D.C., and they're really welcoming. It doesn't matter how old you are.

2. Develop Realistic Expectations and Stay Positive.

Going into a job search with more realistic expectations and making a conscious effort to maintain a positive attitude is another key lesson. These are closely linked because having unrealistic expectations is a common source of frustration, discouragement, and inaction. Zoey, who became an event planner after graduating from Central Michigan University, observes:

My ego and expectations were a lot higher when I started looking after college. Now I'd be more humble. You have to have the ability to get knocked over a few times and just get back up, and not be fazed by rejection. It's an exhausting process.

Myra, who graduated from Brown University as a double major in English Lit and Spanish, adds:

When I graduated I thought success went to those who worked hard and got results. Since then, I've learned it's the most politically savvy and emotionally intelligent—that's who succeeds in the job market.

Ethan needed a job right after graduation because his parents weren't supporting him financially. He adds another caution:

I tell students you need to lower your expectations about pay. If you expect to make $50,000 coming out of college, you're crazy.

Because job searches take longer today, you can be doing everything right, and still you have to find ways to maintain your stamina and confidence longer than you're used to. Taylor learned this during her senior year at the University of Illinois.

I got pretty far in the interviewing process with several companies. When that happened, I'd stop pursuing other opportunities. Then when I didn't get the job, I'd have to start all over. That was the most frustrating part. I'd get really depressed because the process was so difficult.

Sara, a Beloit grad who worked hard to break into the nonprofit world in Chicago, learned the psychological value of sustaining momentum:

Stay positive, but don't get cocky. Just because you have one interview set up, don't stop looking. It's fine to be interviewing at four places at once.

3. Use Career Services More Often.

Taylor, a psychology major who eventually landed a job with an investment bank, reflects on the lessons of her experience:

I wish I had been more open-minded. Learn about the career services your school offers right away. Don't put it off. Even if you aren't looking for a job, start to learn how to do a search. It will help you when you're a senior.

Olivia, a Georgetown University grad working in Internet marketing, echoes this idea:

There's nothing to lose by taking full advantage of your school's career center. They're trying to make you successful after graduation.

And Tobias, who worked as a contractor at Google after graduating from Brandeis University, adds:

I should have gone to career services and identified a short list of companies I'd be interested in. Or, at least, I should have used them to figure out local companies where alumni worked.

Lily wishes she tapped other resources while still at the University of California, Santa Barbara.

I should have talked more with my professors to get a better idea of where I was going. I wish I had used their connections more.

If you're in a school with an understaffed career center, don't hesitate to turn to some of the professors you've connected with. Make an appointment and ask for advice and ideas about career options and others you can talk to.

4. You Have to Know Yourself to Sell Yourself.

The more you know your strengths, weaknesses, values, preferences, etc., the more effectively you can differentiate yourself from the competition. Ethan says he had a rude awakening when he first went looking for a job:

I thought I have this $150,000 education that I'm going to push in some employer's face. But they just wanted to know who I was. They'd never even heard of my college! The most important thing is understanding your strengths before you *go looking for a job. There are plenty of people with an education who aren't getting hired because they don't bring enough to the table as an individual.*

One way you get to know yourself is by trying out different types of work, often through internships and volunteering. Brooke learned this when she graduated from the University of California, Berkeley without any clear career direction.

Some people already know what they like, but if you don't, you're not going to be penalized for having too many different types of jobs on your resume. From the beginning of college, I wish I had gotten more internships. I should have used summers to experiment with different fields, different types of jobs to figure out what I liked.

Potential employers will see your weaknesses, so think through any gaps in your resume before you get questions on them. Lily learned this lesson when trying to sell herself to high-tech companies without any relevant experience.

I got used to hearing "I see you've only worked in art galleries. Why are you here?" And I would explain, "I've learned I don't want to work in the art world, and I agree my major doesn't qualify me for this job. But in the last few months I've tried to get the skills I need, and I'm ready to work in a start up culture." Then I'd elaborate on things not on my resume that were relevant to doing the job and use lingo to show I'd done my research.

When trying to keep themselves viable as job candidates during a prolonged search, successful grads often described the importance of ongoing self-development. After graduating from Colorado College and moving to Minneapolis, Carl benefitted by continually building his skill set, as he struggled to find work in a new city.

One of the keys to keeping my sanity while being unemployed for over a year was staying active by completing the Chartered Financial Analyst exams and volunteering on a presidential political campaign. It's critical to take on projects so your skills aren't atrophying and you continue to grow. That did wonders for my attitude.

5. Be Proactive—Now!

In a world where virtually every hiring manager is distracted by dozens of other priorities, assertively taking action on your own behalf is a critical success factor for any job seeker. Sara experienced this reality when she had to find her second job a year after graduating.

I had gotten lucky with my first job out of college. When I started looking again a year later, I didn't realize how active I had to be. I was sending out tons of resumes and I didn't hear back for months. It was scary. I started thinking, "This is harder than I thought it would be."

There are plenty of opportunities to be proactive; the trick is to make it a habit. Zach saw this senior year at Colby College, as he worked hard to build a network that led to a commercial real estate job.

Plenty of kids at school blamed the economy, but you can easily be proactive. Every school has a great network if you're aggressive enough to use it. It doesn't hurt to go out and meet people.

Sometimes being proactive means explicitly asking for things that may be uncomfortable for you, like names of other people to contact for internships or informational interviews, or asking when a decision is going to be made after a job interview because you're considering other opportunities. Taylor conducted an aggressive job search senior year. She learned you can't start being proactive about your career too soon.

Start as early as you can building a network of family friends and people a few years older than you. Start going online researching companies and job titles. You need to push out of your comfort zone and, eventually treat your search as a full-time job.

Being politely persistent means different things with different employers and industries. Sometimes you'll have to be patient and let the employer's hiring process play out. But other times the advantage goes to the applicant who is both professional and aggressive at pursuing the opportunity. This is true, for example, when dealing with smaller companies. Lucas, who works in television production, learned in his industry repeated contacts are the norm.

As a child, when my parents were teaching me how to get a job in a donut shop, I discovered you had to call up and bug them to show you wanted it more than anybody else. The squeaky wheel gets the grease.

In today's job market, it is much better to be politely persistent than too passive. If you're not consistently proactive you are much less likely to get the job you want. Jon Schlesinger, assistant director of career counseling at the University of Colorado at Boulder, sums it up this way:

One of the secrets is you just have to get started. It doesn't matter if you make a perfect decision. Just pick something and go after it. Whatever you can do, just get started doing it. Whether it's a job search, exploring career options, going after an internship or an informational interview, just do it! Your biggest enemy is stagnation. Talk to people. Try things out.

Follow the lessons here and you're sure to experience a happy ending to your job search. The recent grads in the next chapter describe just what that feels like—to land the job you really want.

CHAPTER TWENTY

"How I Got My Job!"

ow will your job search end? Here are stories from recent grads who remember that moment. I hope your happy ending will feel equally thrilling.

Taking pride in Plan B

Taylor, the psychology major from the University of Illinois, remembers what it felt like to be offered a job as an assistant with a major investment bank in Chicago:

> *I wanted to have a job by the time I graduated, so I spent my whole senior year looking and it paid off! I was going after something different from my psych major, so I knew I had to start earlier. This assistant's job was not a position I saw myself going into after graduating. But now I know this is the industry I want to work in, and I don't have a finance background. I had to start somewhere. I was so excited to get the call from William Blair. It's a long-established, successful company and I knew I could learn a lot. I felt really proud.*

The Theater Major Who Landed at NASA

Ling was an aerospace engineering and theater double major at the Massachusetts Institute of Technology. Her job search wasn't the most challenging, but it did have a surprise ending.

My parents are immigrants from China and expected me to get all As. If they were paying for me to go to MIT, they thought I should study something that would get me a good job. When I told them my major was aerospace engineering, they asked how I could possibly get a job in that. What I didn't tell my parents was that I was also a theater major. I just said I was taking some humanities classes to help with my communications skills.

Being a double major added a lot of stress, but it was necessary for my mental health because the engineering work was so intense. I thought I'd go insane if I didn't do something that didn't have to do with numbers. So I'd jump on stage to rehearse scenes, and then work on problem sets backstage. I was in theater purely for the love of it. I had no intention of acting after graduation.

When I was graduating from MIT, I interviewed with NASA for a job working on flight software architecture. During the interview, all the manager wanted to talk about was what plays I liked and what I had performed in. I thought maybe he knows he doesn't want to hire me so he just wants to fill the time. But later he told me I got the job offer because of my theater degree. He thought it reflected a more wholly developed person with outside interests.

I have since moved to another job in NASA where I work on the kinds of exciting things that aerospace engineers dream about. My current supervisor also hired me because of my acting experience. He said he needed someone with good communication skills, and that's what my theater degree represented. Who would have thought? I debated whether to even list that degree on my resume.

Justice Calling

Daniel was a recent political science grad from Penn State when the U.S. Department of Justice called:

It was August after graduation. I had spent four months in an unpaid internship while I worked a terrible retail job when I got a call from the secretary for the paralegals at the DOJ. She said, "We want to give you a formal offer of employment." I was stunned. The pay was really good. But I didn't say "Yes" right away because I didn't want to come off as desperate. I said, "I'll let you know," but knew I was going to take it.

Unplanned Events: The Downs and Ups of a Successful Search

Zoey was a Central Michigan University recreation major, who had done all the right internships and network building during school. Still, the process of landing a good job was an emotional roller coaster.

After graduation I attended a national convention of Meeting Planners International in Florida, which was great for networking. Back home in Michigan, I sent emails to everyone I had met and added them to my LinkedIn network to help keep in touch. I left Orlando particularly interested in a cool event-planning company in New Hampshire. I met one of the owners but they had no openings. Meanwhile, my internships during school had given me a lot of confidence and I decided I wanted to work in New York City.

I finally found a job opening in the events department of a major New York hotel. I really wanted to work for this company because it was a big name and an opportunity nobody gets. I spent a month at home in Michigan using Skype to do about 15 interviews with people at the hotel. I already knew someone who had an apartment to rent in New York, so I would have a place to live.

In September they flew me to New York for a final round of interviews. Just before I left, I got a call from the company in New Hampshire. They offered me a temporary position providing project support for an upcoming event. I said I'd have to think about it because I was headed to New York for interviews.

When I arrived at the hotel's offices, they said I was scheduled for seven interviews back-to-back that day. Two of my interviewers stood me up, which was annoying. Even more troubling, throughout the interviews people are saying that this job was going to be hell! Here I am ready to take on New York and they're telling me, "You're going to be broke, overworked, exhausted and unhappy. Are you ready for that?"

I actually asked my last interviewer if she would take this job, if she were me. She told me she wouldn't take it. It was heartbreaking to go from thinking this was my dream come true to realizing that maybe this wasn't the life I wanted. After all the work I'd done on the interviews and the whole search process, it was exhausting. I just wanted a job! I didn't want to restart the search.

I flew home to Michigan and made a list of the pros and cons of working for the hotel company versus taking a temporary position in New Hampshire. Then I took a chance. I called the New Hampshire company and told them I couldn't accept something temporary. My contact said she would talk to the rest of her team and see if they wanted to make a full time offer. A few days later my phone rang. I was very nervous. Caller ID showed a New Hampshire number. One of the owners was on the phone and she said they wanted to offer me a full-time job.

I was elated and relieved. It felt like such a long process. I had already made my decision. I was banking on a full-time position. If they turned me down, I probably would have taken New York. But the words just popped out of my mouth, "It sounds great! I can't wait to come." I finally had a job and I love it!

New York, New York

Anna, who had a political science degree from UCLA, was working at a temporary job in Seattle, but trying to land a position in New York in the public-health field. She was turned down when she first applied, but then received the news she was waiting for:

I got an email at 11 p.m. on a holiday weekend. It said I had been selected to be a woman's health advocate for this nonprofit in New York City. I thought, "Oh my God! I'm moving to New York. I got a job! I've never been to New York City, but this is my next adventure. I got just what I wanted!"

Finally—a Good Answer for All Those Embarrassing Questions...

Lily, a UC-Santa Barbara art history major, remembers the day she landed a position as an ad operations manager:

When he called and offered me the job, I took it on the spot. He told me the salary, and I was so elated. I wasn't even thinking that I didn't know much about the job. I just knew I didn't have to be embarrassed in social settings anymore. I called my parents immediately, and they were so excited. Now I had a job and it's what I was looking for. I finally had an answer when people asked me what I was up to.

Answering a "Universal" Call

After graduating from Louisiana State in mass communications, Tyler took a post-grad internship with a Disney public relations department. Anxious about paying off his substantial college loans, he then took a short-lived job as an executive recruiter. This job turned out to be a terrible mistake, and Tyler began frantically searching for a new job.

I had to get the hell out of where I was. Finally, through daily Internet searches I found a position on Indeed.com for a public relations coordinator at the Universal Studios resort in Florida. When I applied I did a phone screen interview with human resources. A week later they had me do another phone interview that was more PR focused. Then I met with two executives in the company, and they said we'll let you know.

I felt I had a pretty good chance, but after five weeks I hadn't heard anything. So I wrote it off as another lost opportunity. Then I got an unexpected call for another interview with the entire team at Universal. I quickly pulled together a portfolio from my past internships because the interview was two days later. I met in a conference room with ten people. The vice president wanted to let his team decide. Were we going to get along?

This was just before Christmas and I wanted this job so badly now. It's hard to enjoy Christmas when you're waiting for the phone to ring. I was a nervous wreck for two weeks. Finally, I got a call. This time they were asking for references. That just prolonged the torture.

Two weeks later I was at my recruiting job, and when I saw the call was from Universal, I ran outside to take it. When they told me they were offering me the job, I was ecstatic! I felt the world fall off my shoulders. I knew this was the real beginning of my career.

When Will You Get the Call?

How will it feel to get the job you really want? See the Special Section following this chapter for more stories showing how recent grads successfully used internships, networking, technology, and interviews to win in today's job market.

 If you are a college student today or have graduated in the last few years, you are starting your career at a unique time in U.S. history. More than 50% of college graduates today are working in jobs that don't require a college degree. Sadly, those without a degree will clearly suffer even more in the job market. A college education (or technical certificate) is becoming the new minimum requirement for being employable in the global economy. But a degree no longer guarantees a good job.

Believe it or not, managers are desperate for good employees. Building a successful career requires you to be proactive, resilient, and focused on adding value in the market. Your primary challenge is to understand what capabilities organizations are looking for and to get some experience that shows you have these skills and the work ethic to develop them further.

Like Laura, Carl, and Maria in the introduction to this book, your journey won't be easy. Long term, however, the payoff of your college investment will only come from using the job search tactics described in this book, seeking honest feedback so you continue to improve, and *never* giving up. For more encouragement, don't miss the stories in the Special Section that follows this chapter.

Your twenties can be the greatest decade of your life. Now there are no excuses—you know how the employment game is played. It's your turn to soar. Go for it!!!

Special Section:

Tales from the field: job search tactics that work.

Stories of Search Strategies That Paid Off

H ere's your chance to learn more from peers who succeeded in scoring excellent post-college jobs.

These stories are drawn from more than 30 extended interviews I conducted with recent grads—primarily liberal arts majors, plus a few engineering and business majors, just so those folks won't feel left out.

As seen in the exhibit at the end of Chapter 1, these grads come from a wide variety of schools in the United States and Canada: from Colby College in Maine to the University of California, Los Angeles and from the University of Florida to tiny Beloit College in Wisconsin. My criteria for choosing people to interview were they had to have: (a) graduated in the last few years; (b) overcome significant obstacles in their job search; and (c) landed a fulltime job they feel really good about.

How to Leverage Internships

These three cases feature students who used internships and volunteer opportunities to gain the necessary skills and connections to standout from the competition. Notice the variety of experiences and the choices they made during and after college that helped position them to land good jobs.

Marco, University of Texas at Austin, Communications Major

From the Tower of Terror to the Houston Rodeo

Many industries are flooded with young people trying to score even entry-level positions. Unless you find ways to get noticed and make connections that lead to opportunities, you'll struggle in highly competitive fields like public relations, fashion, and marketing. Here's how Marco used his internship experiences, along with language and technology skills, to position himself for a coveted PR job at Disney.

My first semester at the University of Houston was pretty rough. I didn't really fit in, and I only completed two classes. I needed a break, so I applied to the Disney College Program and was accepted. I moved to Orlando where I worked at the Tower of Terror, rotating on roles throughout the attraction. I loved my job and made great connections. When I went back to school, I worked really hard and transferred to the University of Texas after two semesters. I continued working at Walt Disney World as a seasonal employee, traveling to Florida during most breaks and holidays.

In Austin, I became director of marketing and promotions for the student television station. I also started a satirical news show, working as on-camera talent and production support.

The summer after junior year, I interned with a film festival in Austin, supporting PR and social media efforts. I got some experience writing press releases, pitching media, and writing for social media channels. Also that summer, I got an unexpected opportunity. I was born in Brazil and we moved to Texas when I was ten. So I'm fluent in Portuguese. One day, a family friend asked if I could host a group of Brazilian agriculture executives who were visiting the Houston Livestock Show and Rodeo. That's a huge event in Texas! I escorted this Brazilian group, delivering their presentations and helping them tour the Houston facility. It was only a week, but now I could say I'd been a translator in a business setting. I had no idea this would have a huge impact on a future opportunity.

During senior year, I left my marketing position at the student-run television station for another internship that I thought would be interesting and different. A local marketing and PR agency was promoting an international innovation conference. I drafted press releases, created social media pages, and managed spreadsheets, which wasn't fun.

I thought it was important to see what it was like working with a variety of clients, audiences, and projects—from customer service at Disney World, to PR for a film festival, to marketing and acting for a TV station, and PR for agency clients. These groups had totally different ways of communicating.

While still interning at the marketing company, I started looking for a job after graduation. I soon realized I probably wasn't going to land a job because the PR agencies I contacted wanted three to five years of experience, which was more than I had. So I started looking for internships again. Disney made me two offers—one in strategic marketing and one in PR. I think I got the PR internship because I played up that I had acted as a translator, which was a huge deal because I knew the position had to host Brazilian media, in addition to supporting some global PR projects.

I also had developed websites and learned to build a WordPress blog in one of my classes. So when Disney wanted someone who could work with websites, those skills turned out to be incredibly valuable. I created a website to showcase my PR portfolio and included a link to the site on my resume, and that was really useful during phone interviews for the internship: I could walk through samples of my press releases, photography, photo captions, and websites.

When I started at Disney a month after graduating, I was beyond excited. It was supposed to be a six-month paid internship, but they renewed my contract. Someone in another PR department at Disney was retiring, so I did my research and learned as much as I could about the position. My boss called the head of the other department and said great things about me. I had several interviews and finally landed this great job as a marketing coordinator!

Faith, James Madison University, Graphic Design (BFA)
& Business Communications (BA) Majors

Making Strategic Choices About Internships to Break Into a Tough Field

If you have a clear career focus, thinking through which internships to pursue will make these experiences count more towards finding a job after graduation. Here's how Faith made those decisions as she prepared to launch her graphic design career.

The summer after my junior year I wanted to see what it was like to work in a large agency. So I applied to a big agency in Baltimore for an unpaid internship. They only chose one of 30 people who applied and they chose me.

In my interview, I talked about my graphic design and communications double major. I'm really passionate about not exploiting women in ads. I talked about that in all my interviews. And I described my church-mission trips to Nicaragua and the Dominican Republic where I was able to work with people from different cultures. That's helped in every position I've gotten.

That summer I worked at the agency two days a week. Because I needed to make money, I also worked four days a week as a cashier at a local upscale grocery store. This agency did a lot of design work for huge clients, so it was very intense. I realized there are a lot of things you can't learn in school. I left there feeling better equipped to work in a professional design atmosphere. The only downside was my boss was doing so much he didn't have time for me.

Because I was a double major I had to take an extra semester of classes, so I knew I was coming back for one more fall semester. Senior year I got a job working 12 hours a week for the university's huge recreation center. I was doing marketing work for them, creating posters and flyers for things like yoga and swim classes and basketball programs. That gave me art pieces out-side my schoolwork, which I could include in my portfolio for job interviews.

I wanted to get experience with a small company during the summer before my last semester. I could have reapplied to the big agency where I had worked, but it would have been more of the same thing. I wanted another resume builder, so I applied to five smaller agencies in Baltimore.

One agency with 35 employees was most interesting to me, but there I was competing against 15 other people for a position. Walking into that interview was the most intimidating thing I'd ever experienced. I'm this little college girl showing them my portfolio, and these two awesome designers are interviewing me. They're criticizing my work in both positive and negative ways.

When they offered me the internship they said they couldn't pay me, but at the last minute they did, so I worked there four days a week. I had a lot more responsibility than at the bigger agency. I actually designed things that went to clients. Working for this designer had such an impact on my design growth. He made time to teach and help me. He was very frank, but not harsh. He taught me so much.

Carlos, University of Maryland, Cell Biology & Genetics Major

From Calcutta to Seattle: Combining Science and Service

If you're someone who feels called to serve others, how do you find out where that calling should take you? Social-action agencies will pick up on your uncertainty and lack of experience if you don't clarify your motivations and strengths. Here's how one University of Maryland science major used volunteering in several very different settings to find his true calling.

During college I got involved in Christian fellowship organizations like InterVarsity and Young Life. I did some spring-break trips to Washington, D.C. and Baltimore to work with the homeless. At the same time, I loved science. I was majoring in cell biology and genetics. My grandfather was always pressuring me to go into medicine. He's really old school. I was adopted by a single mother, but she passed away when I was in high school, so I had been living with my grandparents.

During my sophomore and junior years, I worked with two professors doing research in evolutionary developmental biology. But, near the end of junior year, I knew I loved science and service work, and I wanted to combine them.

The summer after junior year, I did an internship at a Young Life camp in New York. It really clicked for me there. We had groups of campers from the inner city, as well as teenage mothers. I realized I wanted to serve people in the city.

Senior year I looked into Teach For America. There, I could learn how to teach, and I could tie-in science and inner-city work. I also volunteered in D.C. with an after-school tutoring program for inner-city kids, which taught me I wanted to work with middle-school kids. I saw there was so much inconsistency in urban life—absent family members, broken school systems.

But, I still needed to figure out whether I wanted to work domestically or abroad. I was taking five years to finish my science degree, so the summer after senior year I went on a mission trip to India. We were living and working with kids in the slums of Calcutta. I really loved it, even though I was pretty sick the whole time with diarrhea and the flu. I learned from that experience that it's extremely difficult to serve in high-need areas. When I came back, I decided I wanted to work in a U.S. city.

While finishing my degree, a friend suggested I should check out City Year. If I was going to teach, it was a good way to start working in a school system. Even though I had always lived on the East Coast, I had visited Seattle on a road trip and thought I could come to a place like this. So I applied to the City Year program in Seattle, but I got rejected in the first round. That hurt because I thought I had everything set up. I spoke Spanish. I knew how to work with kids, and my interview had gone well. I had so much experience doing a lot of different stuff I thought I'd definitely get it. I really felt entitled to this job because I thought I had done everything right.

City Year said I could put my application on a waiting list and two weeks later they called and offered me a position. I immediately accepted. I was psyched! I had grown up in Baltimore and went to school in Maryland. Now I was moving to Seattle.

Building a Network

Network building is a numbers game: the more quality contacts you make, the more likely your job search will be successful. Here are two stories of students who worked diligently to build successful job-search networks. Notice how the quality of their existing relationships affected the time and effort it took to construct a network.

Carl, Colorado College, Economics Major

Building a Job Search Network From Scratch

Finding a job in a new industry and a new city means building a network to identify opportunities and develop advocates to help you—and your resume—get noticed. Here's how one grad painstakingly built a network to support his successful quest to land a job.

In college, I used my Dad's network in New York City to get an internship. These people had known me since I was a little kid, so it was a much more comfortable conversation than cold calling a portfolio manager and asking for a couple minutes of his time. But I learned to do that when I moved to Minneapolis, my girlfriend's hometown, in August after graduation. A neighbor of my girlfriend's parents gave me a couple of names of people I could talk to. One person I spoke with recommended me for a job at an investment bank. I had two interviews, but didn't get the job.

One night at my girlfriend's house, I was talking with this neighbor who told me to contact Governor Rick Pawlenty's campaign staff. They were looking for an analyst. I emailed the head of the campaign; they brought me on board, but couldn't pay me. The chief financial officer of the campaign was my boss and he promised to help me find a job since he couldn't pay me.

When the campaign ended, he sent out 20 emails to colleagues in the investment management industry.

I was talking to everyone I could think of. I emailed about 150 individuals in four months and probably spoke to half of them, including maybe 45 who I met in person. I got a response from one bank that had me in three times for interviews. But someone in the pool had more experience than me. That's what they would always say. It was frustrating.

When things slowed down, I got the idea to search for Colorado College alumni on LinkedIn to see where they worked. If it was a financial firm, I'd search their company and figure out where they were in the chain of command. I'd read their profile on the website and shoot them an email. If I didn't hear back, I'd give them a call. It's easy to get lost in a pile of email. I learned a call can go a lot further.

One day I spoke to an administrator at my college who had become a friend. He put me in touch with his cousin who is a director at a prominent investment management firm in Minneapolis. We met and he forwarded my resume to a recruiter who interviewed me by phone, but then nothing happened for a couple of weeks. This cousin also introduced me to several friends, and as a result I met a guy from Cargill. I learned about a job opening there for a junior analyst. This guy shot an email to the recruiter, so I got an interview at Cargill for that job, which was really exciting.

Meanwhile, I had joined a squash club in downtown Minneapolis, which turned out to be a great place to meet people in financial services. I met a director at U.S. Bank who passed my resume to recruiters there. They called me at the same time I was interviewing with the investment firm and Cargill. Suddenly in the same week, I had three great opportunities.

Zach, Colby College, History Major

Why it Can Pay to Drive Three Hours for a Cup of Coffee

Breaking into any highly competitive industry is tough and aggressive networking is usually the key to success. Here's how one college senior built a productive network in a city 200 miles away once he realized the limitations of email.

I talked to my friends and saw how their siblings got jobs. In the process, I saw how valuable their networks could be. My Dad knew a lot of people who had done well in commercial real estate, and I had friends who had done great internships in that area. Also, my uncle is in that business so I was able to talk to him to learn about it. I also talked to a lot of Colby alums.

Email is an easier, quicker way to connect with people. A lot of people don't respond to emails, so I'm thinking, "How many can I send this guy?" Once I saw how difficult it was to get an appointment, if someone responded by email and had a phone, then I'd call them. I knew these people were getting thousands of emails, and if I could put a voice next to my name, I'd have a better chance of standing out. Ultimately, though, I was trying to get in front of people because it's hard to emphasize what you bring to the table when you're talking on a cell phone.

I was going to school in Maine and most of the people I wanted to meet were three hours away in Boston. Almost every week in the spring I was driving down to Boston, having coffee with someone for 30 minutes and driving back to school. It definitely got frustrating because I was missing some of the fun of senior year.

I was meeting with people who'd been in the real estate business 20 or 30 years. I'm asking them, "If you were in my shoes, how would you get into the industry?" At first I'd just meet with people and that would be the end of it. But to use my network I had to make a big effort to keep in touch.

I made a spreadsheet that showed who I emailed. This is when we talked on the phone, when we met, and who introduced us. I'd put in their contact information and notes on how the meeting went. Being organized also makes the whole process much easier. I could follow up with emails saying this is what I've been up to. This is whom I've met with since I saw you. It showed these people I'd actually talked to others they'd referred me to.

By graduation, I'd talked to 75 guys in Boston's commercial real-estate scene. And I called on this network throughout my job search. When I had a meeting with a senior executive I'd go through my notes to see who would know this guy.

When I was finally interviewing for a job with this big commercial real-estate firm, the father of one of my friends at school had been best man for a managing director in this company. My friend's Dad, whom I'd met with, called this guy and said, "You're crazy if you don't hire Zach." You've got to use your network for everything it's worth. It's the difference between getting a job and not getting one.

Using Job-Search Technologies

Carmen, Boston University, Public Relations Major

How Social Media Can Jump Start a Career

Here's the story of a Boston University student who has made textbook use of social media technologies to start her career. Carmen was a public relations major who worked her way through school. Growing up in Mexico and rural Nebraska, she is fluent in Spanish and received multiple job offers before graduating. This story shows how she used social media to develop skills, increase her visibility to potential employers, create a viable job-search network, and research companies she is interested in.

The summer after my sophomore year, I took a job at BU as a front-desk attendant in the Events and Conferences department. I knew when I wasn't checking in people, I could work on the computer to learn more about social media tools like blogging and Twitter. I had always loved the idea of LinkedIn. Being from a small town and going to a big-city school, I knew I needed to become more visible.

On LinkedIn, recommendations are really important. The first one I got was from my boss at that front-desk job. The way I always approach it is saying, "Instead of taking time to write a formal recommendation, would you rather give me something on LinkedIn? It's simple and faster and that way I won't have to ask you for a recommendation letter." The next semester I had an internship with a PR firm that must have had 20 interns. I'm not sure how many kids asked, but I just said, "Hey, can you give me a recommendation on LinkedIn, and they did."

I spent my spring semester junior year studying in London where I did an internship for a fast-growing, social media consulting agency. I worked with a lot of social-networking platforms there, including Foursquare, Facebook, Twitter, and Pinterest. They offered me a job, but it would have been too difficult to get a visa to stay. So, instead, they gave me really great recommendations on LinkedIn.

I'm constantly updating my LinkedIn profile and the key words so people can find me. At one point, I went back to all my work experience listings and changed them to be more keyword friendly. Instead of saying, "helped write a blog," I changed it to "create high-quality, relevant content and drive affiliate and email marketing efforts to increase SEO."

Now I'll go on websites of companies I want to work for and look at job descriptions. Then I add skills into descriptions of my previous experiences. Sometimes you don't even realize something is a skill, like email marketing or analytics.

Fall of my senior year, I wrote a couple blog posts about a job fair for start-up companies. Before I attended the fair, I wrote a post saying I'm going to my first job fair and these are some of the companies attending. Then I added brief descriptions of each and linked to their home page. Blogging and tweeting are closely linked. I tweeted about the blog post and included the hashtag for the job fair.

The fair organizers retweeted my blog post so all the companies attending saw it. As a result, I had two interviews immediately. One was looking for a full-time intern and the other company offered me an internship that would turn into a job when I graduated. A couple of months later people running another job fair in New York had seen my tweets and blog posts, and they asked me to come write about their job fair.

Blogging is hard and time consuming, but I use it to build visibility even though a lot of students have blogs today. Learning how to use tools like WordPress Freshly Pressed is also a great way to improve your writing.

It Takes Serious Preparation to Nail an Interview

Finally, here are the stories of two students whose preparation for their intense job-interview experiences had a dramatic impact on their career options.

Luke, Christopher Newport University,
Philosophy & Economics Major

From the Wailing Wall to Wall Street:
The Job Interview That Changed a Life

I was planning to start my master's in religious studies at Hebrew University in Jerusalem after graduating from Christopher Newport University. It was taking me an extra semester to finish because I had a double major in philosophy and economics. But things changed unexpectedly when I was asked to apply for a job as a bank examiner at the Federal Reserve. I had recently participated in a Fed competition for students, so some people there knew me. But I didn't really understand what the job was.

They sent me a package to review and warned there would be a written portion during the interview. I looked through the materials. I didn't know anything about bank accounting. I was really nervous. I went back to my professor and asked if he could help me. So we spent three nights and all day one Saturday studying. At the same time, I was preparing for finals. I showed up 40 minutes early for the interview, planning to review some stuff. But they wanted me to start as soon as I got there. They put me in this high-rise office that was all windows and handed me a pad of paper and a test. It was 12 essay accounting questions related to the packet they'd sent me.

It took me an hour and a half. I was really nervous. There's no way I'm getting this job. When I finally finished, I took a brief break when four people walked in. They handed out photocopies of my answers, and we went through sentence by sentence every essay I wrote. Even the questions where I had no idea, they asked, "How did you come to this answer?" I wanted to say, "I have no clue." Luckily, I threw out a random answer and it turned out to be right. I felt beat up and I'm thinking, you're never going to hire me. Just let me go!

Then they said, "Now we're going to move on to the personality section of the interview." And they asked me to talk about a time when I was in a leadership position. I could answer these questions pretty well, so I started getting more comfortable.

After I'd been there three hours they asked if I had any questions for them. I had a list because my professors said never go into an interview without questions. Finally, I left and just sat in my car for 15 minutes. I was totally drained. I told a friend, "There's no way in hell I'm getting this job."

The Fed interview had been a nice experience, but two weeks after graduating I was preparing to go to Israel to start my master's in religious studies. I was working the cash register at my part-time job at a Barnes & Noble when my cell phone rang. I recognized the number as the Federal Reserve, so I went in the back room. They told me people were impressed by my interview, and they wanted to offer me a job. They gave me a salary range and said I could think about it, but I accepted right on the spot. I kind of regretted that. I wished I had asked for more just to see what they would have said. With one call, my whole life changed! I thought I was going to Jerusalem to go to school. Instead, I'm working in a completely different field, working for one of the most powerful institutions in the world. And I love my job.

Yong, University of Florida, Mechanical Engineering Major

Killing the Interview so it Doesn't Kill You

I didn't think looking for a job was going to be so hard. But five months before graduating, I started to panic because I had no offers. With a degree in mechanical engineering and lots of experience in an on-campus IT job, I decided I wanted to work in project management for a large firm.

My parents are Chinese, but I was born in Venezuela, and grew up in south Florida speaking Spanish. So I kind of speak three languages. During the fall I thought I would get a job easily because I was getting a lot of interviews. I had been going to the Society of Hispanic Professional Engineers conference for three years and when I went in October I got interviews with seven companies. I even passed the second-round interviews in four of them, but I got no offers. I wasn't killing it. So I began to focus on my interviewing skills.

That fall I read a lot of books on interviewing and joined Toastmasters. I'm not shy about public speaking, but I needed to deliver my message better. In undergraduate engineering classes, I almost never spoke. You learn speaking and leadership skills in Toastmasters. The group helps with your grammar. They also helped me make sure I made eye contact and that I had a structure, so I wouldn't forget what I was going to say.

I needed to figure out what I was doing wrong in my interviews. So in January I began recording them when I got to the second round. I used a recorder on my phone, which was in my jacket pocket. I never told the interviewer. Afterwards, I'd listen to it on the plane flying home to hear where I screwed up.

246

My main weakness was when I get excited I speak too fast. When I'm nervous, I tend to skip details. My goal was to improve my breathing and to learn to deliver answers.

Between January and March, I had nine second-round interviews. Out of those, I had six third-round interviews, most of which I taped. From the tapes I knew if I did well or poorly. I learned that if I didn't get enough sleep or drank too much coffee, I didn't think as clearly.

A lot of recruiters just give you fluff in their feedback on your interviews. But I played my tape for my career counselor and she broke down the fundamentals of what I needed to change. It's not how much you know. It's how you deliver it.

In the spring, I got to the third-round of interviews for the General Electric Operations Leadership Program and also for Johnson & Johnson. I got an offer from GE, but I had met a girl during spring semester. So when I got an offer to stay in Florida working for an IT consulting firm, it was a tough choice, but I turned GE down.

It's easier to feel confident you're making a good decision when you have options to evaluate. I know practicing for my interviews gave me those options.

Acknowledgments

I've been dreaming of this book ever since I collaborated with Prof. Shoshana Zuboff at Harvard Business School to redesign the MBA career development course. That was 25 years ago, and helping people find great jobs has been one of my passions ever since.

In reality, it took a lot of people to make this dream come true. I'm particularly grateful to the dozens of young college grads who generously shared their personal, and often painful, job search experiences. This book wouldn't exist without their inspiring stories and reflections on the lessons they learned transitioning from school into the workplace. I am extremely grateful for their contribution to this effort.

I am also grateful to the veteran career services leaders who shared their perspectives on the changing job market for college grads. Thank you to Manny Contomanolis, Megan Houlker, Andy Ceperley, Lisa Severy, Matt Berndt, Jon Schlesinger, Leslie Kohlberg, Denise Dwight Smith, and Meghan Godorov. Other experts in the field of post-college employment have also been very generous with their time and expertise, especially John Wilpers, Quentin Schultze, Sara Pacelle, and Heather Krasna.

This book wouldn't have been possible without the encouragement, discipline, and humor of my wonderful editor Anne Morrissey. She was critical in shaping the manuscript and getting me over the finish line. Cynthia Allegrezza is probably the best copy editor I have ever worked with. She was terrific in our sprint to the end. I also got excellent design help from Priscilla Sturges, Carolyn Kasper, and Nick Zelinger. Together, they brought the book to life and were thoroughly patient and professional in the process.

My spirited research assistant Jennifer Munn played an essential and enthusiastic role in creating this book. I also had much needed, dependable administrative support from Mary Serr. Getting feedback when a book manuscript is still in progress is a great gift. Paul and Leslie Mahoney, Rosa Hallowell, Sara Delano, and my in-laws, Bill and Millie Gladstone, all provided very encouraging feedback. I have never written a book that so many people were anxious for me to finish, just so they could read it. I hope it was worth the wait.

A writer today must also be a marketer, which can be a distracting and time consuming task. Therefore, I am grateful to Prof. Mari Anne Snow and her Marketing 361 class at Bentley University. They enthusiastically took me on as a class project and devoted a good part of their semester to figuring out how to get the message out about this book. You may be reading this only because of the creativity of those Bentley students.

The person most responsible for this book is my amazing wife, Sue Gladstone. Once again, she has patiently and lovingly listened to my dreams, and she continues to say "yes!" I can never thank her enough for giving me the opportunity to do what I love—to write books built on the wisdom and stories of inspiring people.

And among the most inspiring people in my life are our daughters, Anna and Sara. They have just begun to write their own stories. But our daughters face a world very different from the one their parents have known. The ability to find work that is both meaningful and economically sustainable is a challenge they will face for most of their adult lives. Anna and Sara inspired me to write this book because I want their stories of work to be rich and engaging someday. I hope this book will help them fulfill their dreams, just as writing it, has fulfilled one of mine.

Endnotes

Chapter 1

Hope Yen, "1 in 2 New Graduates Are Jobless or Underemployed," The Associated Press, YahooNews.com, http://yhoo.it/IhdnTU (accessed 1/2/13).

Jacquelyn Smith, "What Employers Need to Know About the Class of 2012," Forbes.com, April 3, 2012, http://onforb.es/JKQLJX (accessed 1/2/13).

Charles Blow, "A Dangerous 'New Normal' in College Debt," *The New York Times*, March 8, 2013, http://nyti.ms/13NF9Ud (accessed 3/9/13).

Robert J. Shiller, "Framing Prevents Needed Stimulus," *The New York Times*, September 2, 2012, BU-4, http://nyti.ms/T49Fnf (accessed 1/2/13).

Thomas A. Kochan, "A Jobs Compact for the Future," *Harvard Business Review*, March 2012.

Catherine Rampell, "Majority of New Jobs Pay Low Wages, Study Finds," August 30, 2012, http://nyti.ms/Oe8gFv (accessed 1/2/13).

Catherine Rampell, "With Positions to Fill, Employers Wait for Perfection," March 6, 2013, http://nyti.ms/YOTFD2 (accessed 3/6/13).

"The Road to More Jobs," *The New York Times*, Editorial, July 11, 2012, http://nyti.ms/P1Bo4U (accessed 1/2/13).

David Wessel, "Software Raises the Bar for Hiring," T*he Wall Street Journal*, May 30, 2012.

Peter Cappelli, "Why Companies Aren't Getting the Employees They Need: The Author Follows Up," *The Wall Street Journal*, October 26, 2011.

Donald Asher, *Cracking The Hidden Job Market*, Berkeley, CA: Ten Speed Press, 2011.

"Intern Bridge 2011 National Internship Salary Survey Results to Be Released," PR Web, http://www.prweb.com/releases/2012/2/prweb9173333.htm.

Heidi Shierholz et. al., "The Class of 2012: Labor Market for Young Graduates Remains Grim," Economic Policy Institute Briefing Paper, May 3, 2012, http://bit.ly/YTMvk9 (accessed 3/11/13).

Catherine Rampell, "More Young Americans Out of High School Are Also Out of Work," *The New York Times*, June 6, 2012, http://nyti.ms/VFF8xe.

Derek Thompson, "The Paradox of College: The Rising Cost of Going (And Not Going!) to School," *The Atlantic*, April 2012., http://bit.ly/OOqzpB.

Chapter 2

Cal Newport, *So Good They Can't Ignore You: Why Skills Trump Passion in the Quest for Work You Love*, New York: Business Plus, 2012.

Carl Bialik, "Seven Careers in a Lifetime? Think Twice, Researchers Say," *The Wall Street Journal*, September 4, 2010, http://on.wsj.com/c93l4M.

Chapter 3

"The Value of Career Services," excerpted from *NACE Research Brief: 2010 Student Survey*, September 29, 2010, http://bit.ly/bAcPJt.

Chapter 5

Michael Mauboussin, *The Success Equation: Untangling Skill and Luck in Business, Sports, and Investing*, Boston, MA: Harvard Business Review Press, 2012.

John Krumboltz and Al Levin, *Luck is No Accident: Making the Most of Happenstance in Your Life and Career*, 2nd Ed, Atascadero, CA: Impact Publishers, 2010.

Chapter 6

"NACE Position Statement on U.S. Internships," 2010, http://bit.ly/YTNUqW (accessed 3/11/13).

"The No Limits Job," by Teddy Wayne, *The New York Times*, March 1, 2013, http://nyti.ms/10n4hfV (accessed 3/9/13).

Ross Perlin, *Intern Nation: How to Earn Nothing and Learn Little in the Brave New Economy*, Brooklyn, NY: Verso Books, 2012.

Steven Greenhouse, "Charlie Rose Show Agrees to Pay Up to $250,000 to Settle Interns' Lawsuit," *The New York Times*, Media Decoder Blog, December 20, 2012, http://nyti.ms/12rQyGV (accessed 1/3/13).

Alexis Grant, "10 Paying College Jobs That Look Good on Your Resume, *U.S. News & World Report*, December 13, 2010, http://bit.ly/Y5dUAC (accessed 3/11/13).

Chapter 8

Teddy Wayne, "The No Limits Job", *The New York Times*, March 1, 2013, http://nyti.ms/10n4hfV (accessed 3/9/13).

Chapter 12

Pete Leibman, *I Got My Dream Job And So Can You*, New York: AMACOM, 2012.

Chapter 13

Sharlyn Lauby, "How to Leverage Applicant Tracking Systems to Land a Job," April 28, 2012, http://on.mash.to/YVSEcz (accessed 3/11/13).

Meg McSherry Breslin,"Can You Handle Rejection?" *Workforce Management,* October 2012.

Meridith Levinson, "5 Insider Secrets for Beating Applicant Tracking Systems," *CIO,* March 1, 2012.

Krista Scozzari, "Student Resumes: 9 Steps to a Resume That Avoids 'Black Holes,'" blog post, October 10, 2012, http://bit.ly/VBGFpD.

Meridith Levinson, "New Job Search Service Helps Job Seekers Penetrate Applicant Searching Systems," *CIO,* February 29, 2012.

Meridith Levinson,"Recruiting Software: 10 Ways Job Seekers Can Beat the System," *CIO,* October 26, 2009.

Peter Cappelli, *Why Good People Can't Get Jobs: The Skills Gap and What Companies Can Do About It,* Philadelphia: Wharton Digital Press, 2012.

Karen Siwak, "What You Don't Know About Resume Screening Software Could Be Sabotaging Your Job Search," Ezine Articles, 2012 http://bit.ly/WhwftI (accessed 3/11/13).

Lisa Vaas,"Resume, Meet Technology: Making your Resume Format Machine-Friendly," The Ladders blog, http://bit.ly/XD1MXM.

Chapter 14

Kashmir Hill, "What Prospective Employers Hope to See in Your Facebook Account: Creativity, Well-Roundedness, & 'Chastity,'" *Forbes Magazine,* October 3, 2011, http://onforb.es/qlg8eC (accessed on 12/14/12).

"Managing Your Online Image Across Social Networks," Reppler.com Blog, September 27, 2011, http://bit.ly/raomzc (accessed 12/14/12).

Pete Leibman, *I Got My Dream Job And So Can You*, New York: AMACOM, 2012.

Darren Rowse, "What is a Blog," Problogger.net, http://bit.ly/rgaVQ (accessed 12/14/12).

Ryan Healy, "5 Reasons Every College Student Should Start Blogging in 2009," *Employee Evolution*, January 8, 2009, http://bit.ly/tXoC7x (accessed 12/14/12).

Brad and Debra Schepp, *How to Find a Job on LinkedIn, Facebook, Twitter & Google+*, New York: McGraw-Hill, 2012.

Leslie Kwoh,"Facebook Profile Found to Predict Job Performance," *The Wall Street Journal*, February 21, 2012, http://on.wsj.com/y3PCI5 (accessed 12/14/12).

Miriam Salpeter, *Social Networking for Career Success*, New York: Learning Express, 2011.

Lindsey Pollak, *Getting From College to Career: Your Essential Guide to Succeeding in the Real World*, New York: Harper Business, 2012.

Chapter 15

Martin Yate, *Knock'em Dead Resumes: How to Write a Killer Resume That Gets You Job Interviews*, Avon, MA: Adams Media, 2012.

Quentin Schultze, *Résumé 101: A Student and Recent-Grad Guide to Crafting Résumés and Cover Letters That Land Jobs*, Berkeley, CA: Ten Speed Press, 2012.

Krista Scozzari, *"Student Resumes: 9 Steps to a Resume That Avoids 'Black Holes,'"* blog post, October 10, 2012, http://bit.ly/VBGFpD.

John Wilpers, *"How to: Great Student Resumes in 5 Steps,"* blog post, July 18, 2012, http://bit.ly/V8HjtV.

Chapter 16

Catherine Rampell, "With Positions to Fill, Employers Wait for Perfection," March 6, 2013, http://nyti.ms/YOTFD2 (accessed 3/6/13).

Jenna Goudreau, "Top 5 Interview Mistakes Millennials Make," *Forbes.com*, http://onforb.es/15GdJhj (accessed 3/10/13).

Sara Pacelle,"How to Prepare for a Behavioral Interview," North-Bridge Career Partners blog, January 18, 2013, http://bit.ly/YUA70j (accessed 3/10/13).

Ron Fry, *Your First Interview: For Students and Anyone Preparing to Enter Today's Tough Job Market,* Franklin Lakes, NJ: Career Press, 2002.

Martin Yate, *Knock'em Dead Secrets & Strategies For Success in an Uncertain World,* Avon, MA: Adams Media, 2011.

Susan Adams, "How to Ace a Job Interview on the Phone," *Forbes,* February 7, 2012, http://onforb.es/15ohSHA.

Ming Chen,"7 Deadly Skype Interview Sins," Huffington Post Blog, February 13, 2012, http://huff.to/Z9htEn (accessed 2/16/13).

Matthew Rolston, "How to Look Good on a Webcam," DailyCandy.com, June 6, 2012, http://bit.ly/12RlmTe (accessed 2/17/13).

Time Video, "How to Ace a Job Interview on Skype," http://ti.me/12LGwxw (accessed 3/31/13).

Chapter 17

Princeton Review, *The Best 377 Colleges,* 2013 Edition, New York: Random House, 2012.

"The 13 Colleges With the Best Career Services," HuffingtonPost.com, August 19, 2011. http://huff.to/qzGVGQ (accessed 1/2/13).

Andrew Ceperley, "Chasing Happiness: Is Consumerism in Conflict With Student Career Development?" Working Paper, 2007.

Chapter 18

Anne Kadet, "Job Hunting: When Parents Run the Show," *SmartMoney Magazine,* February 27, 2012, http://sm.wsj.com/x80L0A (accessed 1/14/13).

Mary Jacobsen, *Hand Me Down Dreams: How Families Influence Our Career Paths and How We Can Reclaim Them,* New York: Harmony, 1999.

Lou Carlozo, "Why College Students Stop Short of a Degree," Reuters, March 27, 2012, http://reut.rs/HbsPlh (accessed 1/14/13).

Cloe Madanes, *The Secret Meaning of Money: How to Prevent Financial Problems from Destroying Our Most Intimate Relationships,* San Francisco: Jossey-Bass, 1998.

Julie Lytle and Pegine Grayson, "Preparing Kids for College: Giving Them the Gift of Self-Sufficiency," Whitter Trust Company, Summer 2012.

Jeffrey Arnett, "Emerging Adulthood: What Is It, and What Is It Good For?" *Research on Child Development,* v1 n2: 68-73, 2007, http://bit.ly/VGUAcg (accessed 1/14/13).

Jeffrey Arnett, Emerging Adulthood: The Winding Road From the Late Teens Through the Twenties, New York: Oxford University Press, 2004.

Chapter 20

Allie Bidwell, "Millions of Graduates Hold Jobs That Don't Require a College Degree, Report Says," *Chronicle of Higher Education*, January 28, 2013, http://bit.ly/WbigSM (accessed 2/20/13).

Catherine Rampell, "It Takes a B.A. to Find a Job as a File Clerk," *The New York Times*, February 20, 2013, A1, http://nyti.ms/YehTKj (accessed 3/11/13).

Index

job interviews. *See* interviews
job market, challenges in, 11–18
job requirements, 170–173, 227
job searches. *See also* networking
  attitude during, 214–215
  barriers to success in, 17
  career services role in. *See* career
    services
  competition in. *See* competing for
    jobs
  determining type of work you
    want, 27–29, 47–48, 95–96
  emotions in. *See* emotional states
    in job search
  expectations, 3–4, 23, 33, 53–54,
    214–215
  financial situation influence on,
    18, 35–36, 51–52, 64–65, 87–89,
    199, 203, 215
  focusing your search, 31–32, 37–
    38
  following your passion in, 30–33
  goal setting, 22–23
  identifying job opportunities, 96
  informational interviews in. *See*
    informational interviews
  interviewing. *See* interviews
  job realities and, 33, 35–36
  landing the job. See landing the
    job
  length of, 3–4, 6, 14–16, 22
  lessons learned, 33–36, 213–219
  LinkedIn in, 102, 130–137, 139,
    146, 239, 242–243
  long-term career interests, 33
  non-selection, reasons for, 142–
    145, 154, 166, 178
  online, 141–142, 146–147, 154,
    189
  research activities, 47, 127–128,
    134, 137

  results/how I got my job, 221–227
  resume writing. *See* resumes
  role of luck in, 55–56
  successful strategies, 231–247
  technology in. *See* technology in
    job searches
  time wasters in, 141–142, 154
  values and, 35–36, 51–52, 234–
    237
job titles, 78
job types, 34–35
Jobs, Steve, 28
job-search networks, 66, 97, 99–104,
  107–117, 238–241

K

Keuka College, 183
keywording tools, 127–128
keywords, 14, 60, 125–128, 131, 163,
  242–243
killer resumes, 157–167
*Knock'em Dead Resumes: How to
  Write a Killer Resume That Gets
  You Job Interviews* (Yate), 158
knowing yourself, 39–40, 59, 187–
  188, 216–218
Kursmark, Louise, 158

L

landing the job, 20–21, 49–52, 221–
  227, 231–247
  associate director, educational
    nonprofit, 20, 31, 34
  City Year, middle-school tutor
    and mentor, 21, 236–237
  elementary school teacher, 5, 20
  event planning coordinator, 20,
    223–224
  examiner, Federal Reserve Bank,
    20, 34, 202, 244–245
  freelance TV production, 21, 219

About the Author

Dr. David DeLong is an author, speaker, and consultant who helps individuals develop the skills they need to land good jobs in today's challenging job market. He is also a widely recognized expert on solutions for closing the skills gap, particularly in STEM-related fields.

A former researcher at both Harvard Business School and MIT's Sloan School of Management, he is currently president of David DeLong & Associates, as well as a research fellow at the MIT AgeLab. He has also taught in the MBA programs at Boston University and Babson College.

Also author of:

- *The Executive Guide to High-Impact Talent Management* (McGraw-Hill, co-authored with Steve Trautman)
- *Lost Knowledge: Confronting the Threat of an Aging Workforce* (Oxford University Press)
- *"Buddy, Can You Spare a Job? The New Realities of the Job Market for Aging Baby Boomers"* (Report published by MetLife's Mature Market Institute)

His work has been widely cited in *The New York Times, Fortune Magazine,* the *Wall Street Journal, the Financial Times, CIO Magazine, U.S. News & World Report,* and the *Boston Globe.* He has also been interviewed on NPR's "Morning Edition" and "Talk of the Nation."

For more ideas on how to accelerate post-college job searches, visit www.GraduateToAGreatJob.com.

For information about David's work with organizations on closing the skills gap, managing an aging workforce, and improving knowledge retention go to www.SmartWorkforceStrategies.com.